Don't Try This At Home

Our Life In The Outback

by Anna Johnson

First Published 2016 by Dingo Meeka
PO Box 365, 7 Main Street
Meekatharra WA 6642
Australia
dingomeeka@gmail.com

Copyright © Anna Johnson, 2016

ISBN: 978-1-925952-08-7 (2019 edition)
Published by Vivid Publishing
A division of Fontaine Publishing Group
P.O. Box 948, Fremantle
Western Australia 6959
www.vividpublishing.com.au

 A catalogue record for this book is available from the National Library of Australia

This book is copyright. Apart from any fair dealing for the purpose of private study, research, criticism or review, as permitted under the Copyright Act, no part may be reproduced by any process without written permission. Enquiries should be made to the publisher.

Cover and contents layout edited and designed by Anna Johnson
Cover photograph by Katie Bennett, © Embellysh Photography, 2015
Photograph page 53 © Katie Bennett, Embellysh Photography, 2015
Photograph end pages bungarra © Katie Bennett, Embellysh Photography, 2015
Photograph page 102 © Bithun Wijeeweera 2015
Photographs page 139 © Dave, Splinter & Matty 2014
All other photographs © Anna Johnson, 2011-2016

Many of the pieces in this book first appeared as a monthly column in The Meekatharra Dust between 2012 and 2015 entitled "Don't Try This At Home".

 Anna Johnson lives in Meekatharra, remote Western Australia, with her handsome personal firefighter, Gary Hammer, and highly alert guard dogs Ted and Missy. She has written many articles and news items for The Meekatharra Dust and is the co-author (with her mother) of "The Trailer Diaries" (available on Amazon). She has had work published in Canada and Australia in various small publications and was a winner in the Diamond Valley Short Story competition for her story, "Here Comes The Twister".

In her former city life, she was a film maker and director, best known for her internationally-awarded film, "Seven Days Under Mavis". She also directed many episodes of Neighbours, Home and Away and Shortland Street in New Zealand. Her proudest television moment was directing the Neighbours scene in which Madge died. As Anna likes to put it, "I killed Madge."

Anna also worked for many years as a television commercial production manager, the lunacy of which finally led to her running away from her Melbourne home and enjoying the adventures described in this collection.

THANK YOU

To my family in all its many forms -

My handsome personal harmonica player,
Gary Hammer

Polly, Vicki, June and Angela, for courage,
support, and long distance belly-laughs

My birth family, especially my mum

Joedy and Steve, for test reading and being great mates

The people of Meekatharra

The nuns, the travellers and the truckies

The elders and indigenous friends who helped me understand

AND TO

All the creatures, tame and wild, who have shared the journey:

Honey and Smokey and Sooty
Little Roo
Vincent and Bandit
Boy, Red Dog and Sophie
Ethel and the Chooks
Ted and Missy, who now guard my side
and the skink, of course

This book is dedicated to you, brave Honey.
I miss you every day.

CONTENTS

Where The Hell Is Meekatharra?	p	1
My $70,000 Beer	p	10
Nature - Smash It With a Broom	p	20
Just Turn Left After the Dead Kangaroo	p	23
Meekanomics	p	28
My Fiend The Wind	p	32
W.A. - Where Men Are Men, and .... Ewww	p	35
Domestic Blisters	p	38
Our Trip to the Big City	p	41
Orstraya Day Mate	p	45
In The Ear of the Beholder	p	50
Loose Elastic and a Nice Lie Down	p	53
Would You Like My Brain With That?	p	56
Stay Calm and Grab the Emergency Sock	p	61
Polite Society	p	64
Hammered	p	69
The Finance Retort	p	75
Of Meat and Men	p	80
Meeka Montage	p	84
The Camping Trip - Part One	p	86
The Camping Trip - Part Two	p	90
Of Golf Balls and Balloons	p	95
Mum's the Word	p	99
Booty Scooterin'	p	102
If You're Still Alive in the Morning, Can You Get Me an Icy Pole?	p	107
A Long Time Ago in a Shed Far, Far Away	p	110
More Than Just a Dog	p	115
Fifty Shades of Hot	p	124
When I'm ~~64~~ ~~70~~ ~~95~~ ?	p	129
Inches From Death	p	135
Home Is Where The Toilet Dump Is	p	140
Glossary: Australian Into English	p	147
Recommended Reading	p	153

where is the hell Meekatharra?

Friend: Meegarwhich? Is that a town? Or what?
Me: It's this weeny teeny place in the middle of freakin' nowhere north of Perth or something. We came in off a dirt track, so I'm not really sure.
Friend: What are you doing there? I thought you were going to go live on the beach?
Me: I'm with this guy. We're drinking beer. I just bought a house.
Friend: What? Where?
Me: Here, in Meekatharra.
Friend: Oh my god, are you going to live there?
Me: No no no, just fixing it up and moving on. I'll be out of here in a month or so. They said it gets to like fifty degrees here in summer. There's not even a Bunnings or anything, and everyone seems to be missing most of their teeth.
Friend: Jesus, why the f--k would anyone live there?

If you google Meekatharra, it will tell you that it is a town of roughly (and "rough" is the word) 850 people, of which about half are Aboriginal, located 764 kilometres north of Perth, Western Australia. Wikipedia says that Meekatharra means "place of little water", that the town supports a major mining and pastoral area, is the regional base for the Royal Flying

Doctor Service, and is famous for its rollercoaster boom-bust gold rush history, a story that continues to this day as the miners come and go.

But those are just the facts. The reality is much different. The census doesn't include how many Wiluna mob are camped out on the tank hill during court week, when the population is more like 1000 adults, 7043 children, 879 dogs, 13 abandoned cars behind the pensioners flats, and a goat, unless Richard has shot it, in which case dinner's at six (bring a slab). If the annual Landor races are on, the town's population is Kev, and possibly Ray, unless he's gone down to Gero with Kath, in which case can someone please remember to stop by and feed the dog?

From a city person's point of view, Meekatharra can be described as "Oh my god how do you survive out here?". It's a tiny smattering of houses, pubs and sheds in the middle of the outback, with one small grocery store, a post office, school, caravan park, Kath's secondhand shop, a couple of petrol stations, a veterans' legion, 3 pubs, some government services, and, more recently, Gary's and my "Made In Meeka" local art and tourism shop. By regional standards, we're a busy, well-resourced hub - people drive from stations and remote communities hundreds of kilometres away to shop here. We also have a hospital, volunteer ambulance service, volunteer fire brigade, police station, aged care hostel and the Royal Flying Doctor base at the airport. So basically, with the three pubs in town, you can get blind drunk, have a punch-up, roll your car, get taken to the hospital, be escorted just few hundred metres to the jail cells, and if it's a long sentence, the aged care hostel is just across the creek.

If you aren't familiar with the Flying Doctor service, it's this amazing organisation of nurses and doctors willing to land a small plane in the middle of nowhere to provide you with medical assistance when you've been in a mining accident or run over by your mate Craig on the ATV you made on the weekend out of stuff from the tip even though Pop said not to, you bloody idiots. Other than that, the outback first aid kit is whatever alcohol is left in the esky, and a machete.

Meekatharra is surrounded by canyon-like open cut mine pits due to the gold and mineral mining frenzies that come and go every few years -

you can't see them from the road, but if you have a look on Google Earth you'll be startled. It looks like wilderness when you drive through on the Great Northern Highway, but when you begin to explore the "bush", you soon discover that perhaps every inch of ground has been dug up, walked over, surveyed, lived on and left behind in a centuries-old series of colonial human tides, driven by dreams of wealth, adventure and escape from the safe, upholstered life of the city.

The signs of indigenous habitation are subtle and often hidden, known only to those who remember and protect them. Nomads leave few traces, and it's the elders who pass on the knowledge of places and stories.

We are allowed to sites such as Walga Rock, where we can experience a glimpse of the oldest human past, but that is the exception, and as a non-indigenous person, you will see nothing and know nothing until you earn the trust of an elder willing to "share culture" into your ignorant, sunburned ears. Much of the old traditional knowledge is slowly fading - how to tell the seasons, the time and the weather by the animals, plants and things around you in the bush. How to survive, how to recognise that there is plenty of food out there, that there is water, and more than just survival - that there are stories in the stars above, and in the shape of the land around you, more lyrical and poetic than your science lesson but just as important and accurate in conveying how things came to be, what your place is within this world, and how to understand it.

Sadly, what many of us see as we drive through in our comfortable, fast cars are the lost people waiting for the pub to open, "the abos", the evidence of a shattered culture now all too often welfare-dependent and stripped of dignity, mostly not understood and not wanted, yet offering a wealth of history, knowledge and humour once you get past the layers that have built up from two hundred years of invaders, slavery, genocide, fractured, devastated families and stolen children. Meekatharra, like many small outback towns, is often tolerant but frustrated, broken yet lively, racist out loud and in secret, uncomfortably trying to ignore differences, and getting along in unexpected ways in spite of it all. You'll face challenges you never expected, like being called "a white cunt", hearing an indigenous parent call their child "a little black cunt", or meeting a talented indigenous artist who is sleeping down at the creek and selling paintings so she can buy more alcohol to get herself through the day, then being introduced to her cousin, who might be an articulate, educated woman working for a prime ministerial committee. The contrasts and the culture jolts are a peculiar but constant part of our daily life.

People stop and ask, "Don't you get bored out here?" I have to admit, it was my greatest fear as well - what the hell do you do in a town that's not even a kilometre long, and on Sunday looks like the entire population has been abducted by aliens? As you'll discover in this book, I soon realised that small town life means going to pick up your mail (we have post office boxes, as there is no home delivery), and five hours later sitting down exhausted for a much-needed cold beer after giving old Paddy a lift home, helping Dave find his dog, giving Andrew a hand at the iceworks, showing Raelene where you last saw James or whoever else has wandered off from the hostel, loading Nellie, Pam, Robyn, Don, some groceries and a dog into your car and dropping them off at the shops, pensioners' flats, hospital and Gubby's, then ringing Jo to tell her some tourist has just found an injured wedgetail eagle which you've helped transfer to the back of Phil's ute and can she come and pick it up on her way back from cleaning the court house?

And that's just a normal weekday, not counting your job on top of all that. You also have the volunteer fire brigade, ambulance and State Emergency Service to get involved with, plus the rifle, golf, karts and race clubs, the youth centre, the town gym, basketball, footy, impromptu jam sessions at the pub with the "Bungarra Brothers" (bring your own earplugs), and of course Pool Comp Night at the Royal every Thursday, followed by Fighting And Arguing In The Street.

If you need some excitement and variety, there are always the old standbys such as "Shagging Someone Else's Missus", "Growing A Massive Dope Plant Crop In The Bush The Cops Will Never Find It", "Going To The Tip", and "Driving Home Drunk Via The Back Streets So The Police Don't Catch Me Oh Bugger There They Are" (a surprising number of recreational activities in Meeka involve trying to avoid the police, who are very patient with us and not fooled at all by our poor attempts at evasion).

We have a community garden, quite a few artists, lots of mad prospectors, several Freemasons, Western Australia's last remaining Druid, the traditional Animal Rescue Lady, several Old Blokes, the obligatory grandma that everyone's afraid of, a community-run recycling centre, a swimming pool, at least one crazy lady (most days it's me), an ice factory, an aboriginal community with a small fish farm and regular movie nights, and an outdoor picture theatre which screens a film once every ten years or so when a new person arrives in town and tries to get it going again.

People in Meeka make their own fun, and we have to work together to keep the town running. It's an odd change from city life - out here, if a water main breaks or the power goes down, you could find yourself among the motley team of people helping put it right. I've lent a hand giving someone an X-ray, persuaded an off-duty doctor to treat a run-over stray mutt, guided a lost road train into the stock yards in the middle of the night on my tiny scooter, and been lowered into a mine pit in a rescue basket to save a mate's dog. And I'm a middle aged lady of a "certain girth" - not some daring young athlete! Others in town have similar tales - we all pitch in.

You learn to fix things yourself, and how to do things without money; you ring a mate and payment is in beer, or something handy you found at the tip. A lot gets done with a "busy bee" - tell everyone to turn up with some tools, get stuck into the job, then put on a barbie and grog for everyone afterwards. Job done! Not necessarily the way you wanted it, and those right angles might have come out better if they'd been done before you opened the beer esky, but hey - it doesn't have to look pretty, as long as it works.

In summer it really can reach over fifty degrees Celsius, and the average humidity is often less than fifteen percent - people die out here every year, not realising how dehydrated and overcooked you can get after just half an hour in our outback sun. Standing on the bitumen surface of our lifeline, the Great Northern Highway, the radiant temperature can be over seventy degrees - yet you'll still see our stalwart road crews patiently bearing it, waving you along in your air-conditioned car. Like everyone else, you know them - Debbie, Jacques, Diane, Marty - and wave and yell out a joke as you go by, such as "We've got ice cold beer in the car, see ya!" This typical Aussie humour shows your mates that you care about them.

Contrary to popular belief, it doesn't get cold here at night in summer - it just seems to get hotter. The heat of the day bakes off the ground, and you're grateful for any slight breeze as you lie on your outdoor camp bed with your panting dogs and the lizards and micro-bats that come desperately searching for water. Those of us who live indoors turn our air conditioners on in November and turn them off again sometime in late March. Hell is going through menopause during an outback summer - hot flushes feel like nuclear meltdowns, and you would gladly sleep in a bathtub full of ice (after axe-murdering your partner for not putting the tin opener back in the second drawer).

Winter is cold, even frosty at times, and we sit around our fires of gum tree and gidgie (local tree) logs, complaining about the chill in our bones but glad that it's killed off the billions of sticky, eyeball-sucking flies that plague us for most of the year. We're so used to the extreme heat that we whip out our beanies and jackets if it drops below 35. When Gary and I went back to Melbourne for a visit, my friend June, who was picking us up at the airport, warned us that the temperature was in the mid-thirties. "We'll bring our jumpers," we said, grateful for the advance notice of such chilly conditions.

My friends "back east" swear they couldn't live without cafés, movies, art galleries, culture and shopping - and they don't believe me when I say that there's a different wealth of experience out here. My mother and stepfather worry that I don't have the support network of friends here that I had back in Melbourne - but as I explained, if I need help, all I need to do is walk across the road in any direction. There's something warming about knowing nearly everyone you pass in the street, in waving and saying "G'day", or stopping to talk about ridiculously tiny topics around the freezer section at Farmer Jack's or in the queue at the post office. "Noticed that Billy Nichols has got himself a haircut," someone will say, and we'll spend a good ten or fifteen minutes on that subject. And it's not boring - we'll be laughing and carrying on, and then Billy himself will wander along, and it starts all over again, bringing us closer without any drama or need for anything more. And that's the outback - yes, there's the landscape, but more than anything, it's about people, and your place in the community.

The annual event that defines Meeka, for me, is the Anzac Day service at Paddy's Flat. "Paddy's", as we call it, is run by gruff (with a heart of gold, but don't tell anyone) Vietnam vet Chris Atkin, and is a former mine camp which he now runs as an accommodation centre and retreat for veterans and their families. It's an oasis on the south side of town, and Chris has created a beautiful memorial rose garden around the memorial cenotaph. On Anzac Day, the whole town is invited to come and take part in the dawn service. The fire brigade, police and townsfolk all take part, laying wreaths, then trooping in to "The Mess" for a communal breakfast, generously served up by Chris and the biker veterans. There is something really good about seeing people from all walks of life, adults and kids, all coming together to share a meal and honour those who served.

Sometimes we have to explain to "newbies" how it all works - as I said to a friend from Minnesota once, "The more the Aussies like you, the more they'll abuse you. It's when they go quiet and polite that you need to worry." He was relieved, realising at last why everyone kept calling him various colourful names and "giving him shit", as we describe it. Coming from Canada, even though I've been here thirty years, I've only just started to get the hang of it. When Gary and I see our good friend Steve arrive at the Corner Store for work in the morning, we greet him with "Keep the noise down ya bastard!" People swear like sailors out here, and you don't realise what a foul mouth you've developed until you go to visit your family or friends in the city and they ask when you developed Tourette's.

It's just the way things are out here - no one holds back. I've grown to like it - if you're angry, you just yell and let it out. If it's bullshit, you say so; you might have a full-on blue with your partner or best mate, hurling verbal abuse at each other across Main Street, but you usually patch things up.

Everyone else enjoys the entertainment - you don't need to watch daytime TV soapies in Meeka, you've got the real thing if you just look out the window.

On the other hand, we have a town Facebook page and most days somebody will post "Good morning everyone" and get a bunch of cheery replies from whoever else is up and about. It's like the Waltons (if the Waltons cursed like pirates and were frequently hung-over). Others can be astonishingly up front on their Facebook pages, and it doesn't take much for gossip to do the rounds and expand into increasingly bizarre confabulations. Apparently I was sly-grogging for the aged care residents for a while, and then I died. We had a drink to me at the pub, as I recall.

In the wet season, our town numbers can explode as truckies and tourists find themselves trapped - the Great Northern Highway, which forms our town's Main Street, is the only paved northern route through the middle of Western Australia. I've seen the road trains parked up in every side street during one flood, and one year our town's groceries had to be flown in to the tiny local airport when heavy rains cut off the highway for two weeks. Most of us keep a spare freezer, extra dogs and a pantry full of supplies, just in case. Sometimes the food delivery truck breaks down or rolls over, and it's nice to know that a roast pet or two will stretch the food supply out in an emergency.

There's the whole other world of station life - the incredible men and women who live hundreds of kilometres off the beaten track, living off grid and supplying Australia with its steaks, a lonesome but not always lonely life rich with generational history, battered old hats and a down-to-earth no-worries self reliance that you wish was still alive in the towns and cities. For a good read about the lighter side of station life, get hold of a copy of Raelene Hall's book "Legitimate Bush Woman" via her website, www.outbackwriter.com. She lives a couple of hundred kilometres north of us at Ned's Creek Station - just a short drive up the road for locals!

There are the fly-in, fly-out miners and regional workers, medical visitors and mine camp caretakers, the itinerant prospectors who occasionally vanish forever into the baked red vastness, the anthropologists and geologists and other ologists, travelling racehorse owners, backpackers, insane Japanese cyclists, people crossing Australia with a wheelbarrow, wheelchair, roller skates, ride-on mower, farm tractor or some other mad form of transportation, raising funds for various causes; we have Sudanese refugees, remote area road crew workers, descendants of the Afghan cameleers and the Batavia shipwreck, an unknown number of escaped criminals, a mad prospector living on a "patch" behind the hospital - the diversity is amazing, endless, funny and weird.

We have people here from Sweden, Germany, Ireland, Taiwan, Thailand, Tonga, England and all over Australia. Some stay behind closed doors as much as they can, while others embrace the outback life, wrestling with the Aussie vernacular and valiantly greeting everyone with a meticulous "Good-day mate", horrified by what we call "food" but grimly whacking on the tomato sauce while discovering that despite the locker-room humour, the rough-as-dogs-guts manners and the ear-burning language, you're accepted here for who you are. The person you first dismissed as a scruffy no-hoper will suddenly appear at your side to help put out a fire, or bring you some roo meat when they hear you're out of work, and when you need a hand or a shoulder to cry on, all you have to do is step outside your front door to see that you are surrounded by these oddball, eccentric and diamond-in-the-rough people you call your mates.

my $70,000 beer

I stopped in Meekatharra in October 2011 with a friend to have a quick beer (this in itself is a ridiculously long and unsuitable story, which I think it's best not to go into right now). Five days and quite a lot of uncharacteristic drinking later I woke up to discover that the beer had bought me a house in Main Street, a short staggering distance from the Royal Mail Hotel, with excellent views of passing road trains and just a stone's throw from the pensioners' flats. Location, location, location!

I'd been living and travelling in my bus for nearly a year with my faithful travelling companions, Honey the foxy-chihuahua cross and Smokey, The Cat Who Walks, having abandoned my five-star film industry lifestyle in Melbourne to search for adventure and real life away from the insanity of the city. The plan was to not have a plan, which is still working out brilliantly.

My adventures as a roadrunner could fill a novel - towed off the Nullarbor, playing kelp chasies with young seals, living off fish and calamari, shacking up with a mad roo shooter, kidnapped by a charming Aboriginal mine worker, living off stock market trading while camping on the beach, working as a short order cook at a remote roadhouse, fossil hunting in the Flinders Ranges, feasting on roast bungarra, living life instead of slaving to buy more "stuff". You can read a hygienic version of my bus adventures (mum toned down some of the naughty & controversial bits) in "The Trailer Diaries", which my mum put together, based on our blogs one year when everyone in our family went a bit mad and ran away from home - it's available on Amazon (the book, not our family, although I think Mum would be open to offers on us kids).

Meeka sprang its own surprises on me from day one, and I soon found myself busy taking damaged fruit & vegies out to Ken's pigs at Sherwood amid the chaos of The Great Truck Rollover, helping fight the house fire at KD's, wrapping Christmas presents at the aged care hostel, chasing kids down the street as they tried to make off with stuff from the bus, and lurking in the beer garden at the Commie, lying in wait for unsuspecting tradies who could help me with repairs at the house.

Right from the start I felt welcome, with much help from people like Brian & Christine, Sunshine, Hazel, Patreen, Damien, Mick, Kev, Ray and many others, including Cam Harvey, the captain of our local fire & rescue brigade at the time, who kindly donated a spare dog, spare chickens (chooks, they're called in Australia) and a spare bloke to my household. This is how it happened:

The first week he was helping me at the house, Cam said (in his thick Scottish accent), "Och, ye could doo wi' a bigger dog. I've got a spare one, I'll bring 'im roond." Sure enough, he brought Boy, an enormous boofhead mastiff something-or-other Aussie pig-dog who promptly wallowed in the runoff from the busted greywater pipe and then shook all over us. He was a big sooky thing who quickly settled in with Honey and Smokey and me. "He'll be a greet guard dog for ye," claimed Cam as Boy snored and farted on the back verandah in one of his 10-hour-long comas.

A few days later Cam said, "Weel, ye'll be here a while wi' these repairs, ye may as weel have some chooks to gi' ye some eggs, we've got some spare ones, I'll bring 'em roond." So, next day, he brought some chickens, who settled into the tomato plant boxes and glared at Smokey.

A few days after that: "I reckon ye'd like me mate Gary, I'll send him roond." Sure enough, a tall handsome fellow turned up on my doorstep at exactly 7:00 pm on Friday December 23rd, took me out for dinner, and we haven't been apart since. As I like to joke, I can thank the Meekatharra fire brigade for donating a dog, some chooks and a spare bloke to my household - and just when I thought I'd opted for a simple life!

As Gary and I got to know each other, we discovered that he used to work across the street from my old apartment in St. Kilda, and that we had both gone to the same tiny café in Chapel Street almost every day for years - so we would have been within a few feet of each other many times in Melbourne. Even more bizarrely, it turned out that I'd had an internet date with a bloke he used to live with, and Gary even remembered him coming home from the date saying "I blew it!" (inappropriately early groping attempt, as I recall).

And the coincidences didn't end there - we also worked out that he'd been the RACV on-call mechanic for my suburb back in the 90's, and that he'd jump-started my old Cortina one morning. We're not big believers in fate, but our story sure makes you wonder - crossing paths for nearly twenty years in the city, then actually meeting thousands of kilometres away in the middle of nowhere thanks to the match-making efforts of a Scottish-Gypsy former Foreign Legion soldier in the local fire brigade. You couldn't make it up if you tried.

In the "weird or what?" category, I had another past connection to Meekatharra - many years ago I organised a film crew to shoot a TV commercial for Telstra out at Hillview Station. Although I didn't come out for the shoot myself, I spoke to many locals on the phone, trying to contain my city dweller horror at the lack of vegan food options or - gasp - fresh lattés. At that point all I knew about the outback was what I had seen in the movies "Wake In Fright" and "Mad Max". Some of the people I spoke to on the phone actually sounded like characters in Mad Max, laughing in a slightly sinister way when I asked if they had vegetarian options on the hotel menus, which consisted of "Meat, Meat, Meat, Chips, Meat and Stack Of Meat Five Different Animals (with chips)".

"Don't tell them you're vegetarian," I advised the art director. "They'll kill you." And probably eat you, I thought. It seemed like a place where anything could happen, and when the camera assistant rang to tell me that it was fifty degrees and they were wearing gloves to prevent their hands from being burned by the metal film equipment I thought, who in their right mind would live out there?

So I was just going to do the house up and move on, but I somehow fell in love with all the madness, unpredictability, characters, stories and the way that work and social life merge together during the course of each day. Before long, I had joined the fire & rescue brigade, got a job at the aged care hostel and had Bob at the Commie remembering my name and what I liked to drink - a sure sign of being accepted. Meeting Gary was the icing on the cake, and I began to realise I wasn't leaving anytime soon.

If you don't have a Gary, I strongly recommend getting one - not only is he my handsome personal tour guide to the lesser-known pockets of our local ghost towns and swimming holes, he's also my Meeka mentor, with helpful tips ranging from 'How Not To Die Just A Few Kilometres From Town' to 'That's Where A Goat Got Stuck Under The Court House Back In The 1960's'.

I recall the moment I realised just how small Meeka is. Kev and Ray had just arrived to put up my front fence; I rode up to the shops on my bike, and as I walked into the hardware ten minutes later someone said "Your new fence is looking good, love!". I had to laugh, but I also thought, "I really like it here."

One of the first things I had to learn in Meeka was how to get directions (nobody uses the phone here; you just go to the pub on Friday nights to find a tradie, or drive around town until you see who you're looking for). Here's how a Meekatharran will give you directions:

"Yer mate it's just round the back of Norm's old place next to where Baz used ter keep the ute he got off Millie after she run off with Grunter, past where the green shed was next to where Wazza's house used ter be before it burnt down then I think Jay bought the place or bloody wotsisname with that dog his missus got off Ken that bit Matty in the leg, anyway yer can't miss it."

I would be riveted to the spot, burning with questions. Why would Millie run off with someone called Grunter? How did Wazza's house burn down? What kind of dog did wotsisname have and why did it bite Matty's leg? Who was Matty? What happened to the dog? It was more compelling than television, and I would drive around for ages, utterly confused. "I'm looking for Grunter's place," I would say. "Oh, no I'm not, I mean I'm looking for that place that was next to Grunter's place...or...um...look, if you see Tom tell him I'm looking for him. I'm at the yellow house with the slate blue fence, next to that empty lot on the other side of the child protection office, no, Ev's old place, next to where...oh, for god's sake, tell him I'll see him round the pub sometime."

I buckled down to fitting in, and getting a job. I hadn't had a job for something like thirty years, having been working freelance in the decadent world of TV commercials, so it took a bit of getting used to. For some reason, the aged care hostel decided that the best person to do the Meals On Wheels deliveries each day would be me, a former Canadian with absolutely no idea, no map and no GPS, in a town that had no street numbers on the houses and a wildly nomadic residential population. I asked for a list of delivery clients, and was given a piece of paper with things like "Aunty Dot McCleary Street or shops, Old Bill, Don (near Ronnie's house), Ben at aged care or might be down at the creek" written on it. So I decided to just drive around asking people in the street, sometimes giving them a lift in exchange for directions. This is how I met many of the aboriginal locals.

It was quite entertaining, and I learned a lot. "I have to deliver a meal to Trevor," I would say. "Yeah, you go dat way," my companion would point. "Ey, ey, slow down, dat old Harry, we ask im. WHERE PAM HARRY?" "Pam?" I would ask. "Uncle Trev, sometimes he with Pam," my companion would helpfully explain.

Old Harry would then come over and lean in the window. "You got any smokes sis?" My cultural advisor companion would turn to me. "Ere, you give im some smokes, give im a lift," I would be told. No worries. "Turn ere, we ask where Pam."

I would obediently follow instructions while my passengers shouted out the windows. "WHERE PAM?" Various people would turn and shout back. "SHE GORN GERO MATE! TREV AT UNCLE RON'S! YOU GOT ANY SMOKES?" Sometimes a person standing over a block away would see us meandering along and just point in the right direction.

Eventually we would find Trev, give him his lunch pack, and it would start all over again as we searched for our next wandering senior citizen.

Soon enough I was able to do the rounds on my own, although at first I made the classic mistake of asking for directions or help the way you normally would. "Excuse me, do you know where I might find Uncle Trevor, or Pam, please?" This would get blank looks, until I realised - silly me! - I was doing it all wrong.

"WHERE PAM?" I would yell.

"SHE AT WINGO'S! YOU GOT ANY SMOKES?" someone would yell back.

Finding myself in a mostly aboriginal community was by turns alarming, hilarious, great, depressing and just so different from anything I'd experienced, even though I've lived in Africa and travelled to quite a few places, rich and poor. But I'd never, in over twenty years of city life in Melbourne, met an indigenous Australian, except for the time we had Cathy Freeman on set for a TV commercial, and I had no experience at all of Australian aboriginal culture, apart from what appeared occasionally on the mainstream media.

Coming from the city and a generally left-wing arty farty academic and world travelling background, I was keen to be inclusive, open minded and ready to embrace whatever this new culture would have to offer.

Within three months, however, I had become cynical and horrified. Even in some of the poorest parts of Africa, I had not seen people treat their children and animals so badly, or live and sleep amongst their own refuse. As a home and community care worker, I saw a side of Meeka that I think would shock even some of the locals, and would definitely have any tourists or city folks running screaming. For my indigenous friends and other aboriginal readers, please bear with me for a page or so - I want to talk about what I saw, my first impressions, before we move on to the bigger and better picture.

What I saw at the pensioners' flats area and many of the houses in Consols Road was rotting animal meat in the yards, toddlers in nappies left to wander the street at two in the morning, dogs absolutely covered in ticks, often with a dangling, untended broken leg, broken glass and alcohol cans everywhere - these places looked like a war zone, and on Friday and Saturday nights that's what they sounded like. The aged pensioners' flats were indescribable; it took a strong stomach (and a stout stick to ward off the snarling, hungry dogs) to go in with deliveries of medication and food. People were welcoming, friendly and great to talk with at all these places, which made it all the harder to understand.

When I asked about the rubbish and the damage, people would blame 'Wiluna mob', or the younger people, mostly young men, who would come and 'humbug' the older folks for their pension money, then hang around drinking and making a mess. At one point, some visitors left a baby behind! One bloke was sleeping in a bed with a packet of maggot-infested meat, and every day kids were ripping panels off the fence to use them for sliding down the tank hill. No one stopped them.

It still goes on as I write. Wrecked cars, wrecked houses, screaming and swearing at all hours, and hearing adults loudly call their children "little black cunts" in the supermarket and in the public street. If you're shocked reading this, try living with it. Try being a normal aboriginal person who doesn't act like this, but has to put up with the daily prejudice that inevitably - and understandably - builds up.

There are groups of indigenous people sitting in the street in front of the pubs every morning, waiting for the noon opening. You see people pushing prams full of the insidious "red cans" (Emu beer) along the street on 40-degree days, with the toddler struggling along in bare feet on the bitumen or across the sharp spiny weed-ridden vacant lots that form the "back way" to the public housing areas, being yelled at for crying at the pain in their tender little feet. When you arrive in Meekatharra, that's often the public view you get of aboriginal people.

It's upsetting, confusing, awful and everything else you can think of. You feel like doing something about it, but what? Where to start? There are literally millions of dollars spent each year to address these problems, and thousands of people working hard to help, but in my view there is no amount of money or support that can fix the brain of a four year old child who is sniffing petrol down at the creek night after night.

City people freak out; my friends freak out. "But can't you...why don't people...aren't there any programs to help...?" My answer is, Come on out and experience it for yourself, and tell us what can be done. Have a go. I guarantee you will end up angry, confused and disillusioned too, because this is a problem created by destroying human beings on a vast cultural and personal level, making them welfare-dependent in a society that is sinking into a self-created abyss of television, mobile phones, soft drinks and junk food, then turning around and saying, "Get your shit together, loser".

My aboriginal friends and workmates have given me some of their insights into the problems here. I'm not going to do it justice - there's no justice to be found in any of it, it's a mess - but here's a nutshell version: Meekatharra is a kind of "no one's land" in terms of indigenous history. It overlaps multiple skin groups, and therefore it can develop into a conflict zone. As one person put it to me, it's a "mongrel place".

On top of that, you have the exhausting, horrible over-and-over again history of colonial devastation, things that would make you throw up, and there are still people alive who remember it first hand. And like the white suburbs of Australia's major cities which have the same kinds of welfare dependency problems, all you need to add is a lifetime diet of alcohol, cigarettes, soft drinks, two-minute noodles, television and Facebook, and you get futureless, frustrated and angry people, teenage girls having babies so they can collect the $3000 baby bonus, and a whole bunch of generational social problems.

But what you don't see when you drive down the main street are the normal people, the aboriginal people who simply get on with being themselves, forming an indigenous and integrated normality away from the welfare behaviour. You might not see them straight away when you drive into town, because they're at work, at school, looking after grandparents and children, working on their paintings, grading the roads, working at the hospital and the youth centre - just like everyone else.

If you do come to visit, stop and talk with the people you see waiting for the pubs to open - you'll be surprised when you discover that many of them are just older locals who don't have much else to do. They're slowly losing their place in their community, but they have some wonderful personal stories to share, and they've achieved things that deserve our respect. I've seen our travellers and tourists looking nervous around aboriginal people, and some of our rougher-looking outback folks - but don't be scared. All of us are people, just ordinary people, living in an extraordinary place, and everyone's got a tale to tell if you have time.

It's riveting to talk with the older locals about their childhoods of traditional bush living, to hear stories about the lives of mission girls, to go out looking for bush tucker and learn how to make traditional ash for chewing tobacco or how to tell time from the "bush clock" flower. Old Aunty Kay remembers the last train from Wiluna, and Richard will tell you some dreamtime stories and show you a photo of him at fifteen, in a clean white shirt, black dress trousers and bare feet, being presented with an equestrian award by the State Premier.

There's the Mongoo girls, Mickaela and Janine, who at only 18 are national rodeo champions (and who have battled some serious personal hurdles that would leave most of us crying on our knees). If you drive down Oliver Street, make sure you wave to Nellie, who remembers "coming in from the desert" to live on a station at the age of ten and keeps everyone laughing with her cheeky sense of humour.

You might also run into Ralph and Brandon, firefighters and all-round awesome blokes, Beryl and her family, who are amazingly talented artists, good old George who saved the young policewoman's life at the infamous Royal Mail Hotel stoush, Elaine, our take-no-crap matriarch and ambulance driver, Rhonda who's an advisor to the federal government and just a wonderfully happy person to be around, and of course there's Andrew and Janine and Robert and Alicia, plus Uncle Shorty and all the others, who keep Buttah Windee community and Meekatharra thriving with art, family and culture, standing strong for the young people of our town.

There's Gloria and Charmaine, working with Mission Australia and still finding time to create wonderful paintings, Michelle with her stunning hand-painted furniture, James who collects ochre and corkwood ash for his traditional paintings (which smell like the kangaroos that live in caves where the ochre comes from!), Steve and Heather and Brian and Maxine and Bomba and Tristan and Jody and Raelene and Helen and Phillo and Chriso and Daryl and Alison and Glen and Byron and Rocky and James and Shelley and Bevan and Betty and Deanna and ... please forgive me if I've left anyone out, there are so many great people here, so when you drive down Main Street and see "a bunch of abos" sitting waiting for the pub to open at midday on a Monday morning, just remember that what you see is not necessarily what you think it is.

If you want a great read that gives you more insight into some of WA's indigenous experience and day-to-day life, get hold of "Elephants in the Bush and Other Yamatji Yarns", by Clarrie Cameron - humble, funny and full of anecdotal detail. The TV image of outback Australia is all too often the laconic white bloke in the Akubra, but if you come out here you soon discover that outback people are all colours and backgrounds, and a lot of them are - gasp - women. It's diverse, mixed up, weird, funny and amazing.

I once embraced the bling & fling of the city, enjoying a lifestyle that many people would envy; it seems alien, distant and crazy now. Life here is filled with endless delights - the vast horizon and star-filled night sky, the ever-changing red, orange and sage tones of the bush, the majestic wedgetail eagles and budgies like bright green jewels, the ghost towns and the sound of the wind in the acacias, far from any human noise.

Morning rambles with the dogs bring daily pleasures - the oasis of the Afghan camel soak, tiny wildflowers coming into bloom, a rusting horseshoe from olden days, strange gigantic mining equipment travelling past on the road trains, emus running across Main Street like panicking feather dusters. Our sunsets and night sky take your breath away.

On our return trips from Geraldton, Gary and I both heave a sigh of relief as we pass the sign outside Yalgoo which says "The Outback Starts Here". The horizon opens up into forever, the foolishness of the city evaporates, and as the Commercial Hotel, heat-battered bougainvillea and scattered red cans along Main Street come into view I think, "Home."

Nature - smash it with a broom

As summer approaches, frying our eyeballs and baking the wet clothes into instant cardboard on the washing line, Gary and I look forward to relaxing in the breezeway, playing our favourite games, such as "What Hideous Gigantic Insect Is That?!", "Oh God Get It Off It's In My Hair!" and "Now I've Made It Angry".

I arrived in Meeka a year ago, an innocent city gal, eager to embrace the many wonders of the outback as promised in the West Australian tourism websites, but they didn't mention the harsh realities, focusing instead on useless information about wildflowers, failing to warn city folk of the nightmarish multi-legged encounters that await, and irresponsibly not advising that you need to pack a flamethrower. In Canada, we only had to worry about bears, rattlesnakes and angry elk, so I wasn't prepared for the fanged foot-long centipedes, lurking scorpions or the dreaded Meekatharra Cockroach; I had to learn the hard way.

I had only just moved into my house in Main Street, and Trenny was round tidying up some of the electrical wiring; he popped his head up into my roof cavity, then grimly descended the ladder, looking a bit pale. "You might want to bug-bomb the place," he advised as he backed hastily out of the house.

I chuckled. "Oh, I'm sure there are a few critters, not to worry."

I grabbed my single can of Mortein, gave the kitchen cupboards a quick blast, and sprayed a bit in a hole in the laundry wall just for good measure. All done!

Suddenly the kitchen exploded with dozens of enormous panicking cockroaches pouring out of the cupboards, and to my horror I could hear untold numbers of them RUSTLING IN THE WALLS. I don't ever, ever want to hear that sound again. I rushed up to Farmer Jack's, bought all the bug bombs they had, flung them into the house like grenades, and ran.

Within seconds there were hundreds of them fleeing the house. As I drew upon the time-honoured city-gal emergency response skills of Shrieking and Flailing Wildly With A Broom, trying to defend my bed on the verandah from the writhing hordes, my friend's son Jack popped in to say hello.

Jack, who is 12, looked calmly at the writhing ghastly scene and said "Cool." We took up a defensive position near the bus, chatting and screaming as Jack crunched them underfoot ("Awesome") and I popped off rounds with a backup spray can. As the first wave of roaches subsided, we stood outside the sliding glass door to watch the skin-crawling carpet of horror inside the kitchen. Dozens of dying cockroaches scrabbled helplessly at the glass. You could almost hear their tiny, pathetic screams. We laughed. Then I remembered that I should probably set a good role model example for young Jack with some kind of "all creatures deserve our respect and cockroaches are actually quite interesting" comment but what came out was "Ha ha! The poison is dissolving their central nervous systems!", reinforcing the fact that I am perhaps not an ideal person to leave unsupervised around children.

By the time I'd swept up the bucketfuls of twitching, dying roaches, the part of my brain responsible for Fear Of Unreasonably Large Creepy Crawlies had been burnt out from sheer overload, and I was ready to accept the grotesque species diversity of Meekatharra's summer insect population. At first it seemed interesting and novel - look, a stick insect! And here's one that looks like a leaf! Isn't nature amazing? Then the Big Green Thing moved in.

It was like a locust on steroids, as big as a cogla fruit (bush banana), a beautiful creature in delightful shimmering shades of green. It wouldn't leave the bedroom, and Gary said "I imagine the poor bugger's getting hungry just sitting there." I opened a window while Gary gently lifted it with one finger, marvelling at its delicate colours. "Come on mate, let's get you--- AAGH! BASTARD'S BITING ME!"

A violent blur of man versus insect filled the room as Gary wrestled with the enraged monster. We cornered it near the bed and beat it with a broom, but it just laughed and made a rude gesture with its feelers, so I smacked it flat with a boot. "I sure hope it's not one of those bugs that injects a massive dose of necrotising poison which gradually eats most of your flesh away," I said reassuringly to Gary as I poured betadine into the bone-deep fang wounds in his finger. We had a stiff drink, wildly sprayed seventeen cans of Mortein around the house, and went to bed in a thick protective coating of Tropical Strength Aerogard.

I learned much during my first Meeka Insect Season. Nature is rich and rare, offering a plethora of wondrous creatures which make our planet a healthy, thriving biosphere. We all need to learn to live with our insect neighbours, sharing in symbiotic harmony. Therefore I'm happy to accept that insects are a part of nature's plan, as long as they accept that our plan is to respond with an arsenal of weapons-grade insecticide, flame-throwers and of course a .222 for the larger insects.

Now all we have to worry about are snakes, dingos, floods, heatstroke, bungarras, and of course the worst of all, weekend takeaway alcohol restrictions. You just don't get this kind of excitement in the city.

just turn left after the dead kangaroo

One of my aged care community clients was an old bloke living "out at the racecourse". Confident with my new Meeka echo-location skills ("WHERE GEORGE? YOU GOT ANY SMOKES?"), I headed out on the Wiluna road northeast of town and turned on to a dirt track for the historic Meekatharra racecourse. At least I knew Meeka well enough now not to confuse the raceCOURSE with the raceTRACK. Naturally the raceCOURSE is on the northeast side of town, for horse racing, and the raceTRACK is off the airport road on the southeast side of town, for car racing. You idiot.

By now I considered it perfectly normal to spend most of my work day utterly confused, lost and mystified, so going out to a racecourse to drive around looking for some bloke I'd never met living in a shed with no address was a relatively calm and orderly task compared to what most mornings were like ("WHERE PAM? WHERE TREV? WHERE BEN?").

As I headed for the racecourse buildings, I pondered the usual questions that accompanied most of my duties. Why was the old bloke living out at the racecourse? Was he in a house, a humpy, a caravan, or what? ("He's in one of the sheds, off to the left, or maybe the right, by some trees"). I was picking him up because his driver's licence had been cancelled due to age-related medical conditions, so I figured I just needed to look for a vehicle.

I wandered around the racecourse area along a series of baffling, labyrinthine dirt tracks, entertaining the horses who were watching me drive back and forth. I swear they were laughing. It was all bush, with scattered old tin sheds and the usual "don't throw that out, it might come in handy" scrap piles. By sheer accident, I came upon a fenced compound of beautiful flame trees, a tired-looking ute parked out the front and a painstakingly hand-lettered sign that read

The sign was right, and I hopped from one foot to the other to shake off the sudden frenzy of ants swarming on to my boots as I knocked on a fortress-like corrugated tin gate and called out, in time-honoured Aussie fashion, "Cooee!". After fifteen or twenty minutes of staggering noises, rattling chains, huffing and puffing and mutterings of "is it this one or... ...bloody hell...this one...no...crikey...", the gate groaned open.

And so I met George, and my soon-to-be new home. It was a ramshackle collection of unlined tin sheds within a fenced garden setting, and old George wanted to sell. The poor man had been living there for sixteen years, but his worsening diabetes and myriad health problems meant he couldn't run the genny or do any of the other essential chores needed to live in this semi-off-grid compound, or "camp" as we call them out here. So he was living in the dark with a bed full of mice, and only a Coolgardie safe hanging from the verandah beam to keep his milk and vegies cool in the brutal summer heat.

Rough and run down, it was nevertheless a charming, peaceful retreat surrounded by lovely big trees and nothing but the sounds of the birds and the bush, and George, who couldn't seem to stop talking. It must have been lonely out there, and I felt sorry for him, although after an hour of hearing about things like why he liked using five mill screws and how many rivets he used to repair the gas fridge door I stopped feeling sorry and just wanted to knock him out with a blunt instrument.

He didn't want much for the place. I dropped him off at the hospital for his appointment, then raced off east in my old bus to find Gary, who was grading the Wiluna road; I found him eighty kilometres out, somewhere near the Killara Station track. "Old George wants to sell his camp! He only wants 7500 for it!" I yelled out the bus window.

"Just buy it!" yelled Gaz.

So I did, and to cut a long story short, we moved in a month later, after helping George shift into the aged care hostel in town. The camp, or hovel as some might call it, was on common land, and we didn't own anything but the actual buildings and chattels; it was an unspoken squatting arrangement, typical in the outback. Sadly these eccentric off-grid dwellings are slowly giving way to the tentacles of bureaucracy, greedy for dollars and control.

As I came to learn, having a "camp" was nothing unusual; nearly everyone had a little spot somewhere on the outskirts of town or way out bush - it might be nothing more than a fire pit and a few chairs, but could go all the way to being a makeshift house and outbuildings, complete with handmade stone swimming pool, all running on generators, wind power, solar panels and sheer ingenuity.

My friends in the city couldn't get their heads around it. "You're living in a SHED?" they asked. The idea of living without town electricity or utilities was appalling. Miraculously, our "Bush Camp", as we came to call it, was connected to the racecourse's town water supply, but everything else was DIY. Gary soon had solar panels and old car batteries hooked up, and a generator that we turned on to run the washing machine when we needed it. We turned the fridge on for a few hours every day just to cool the food down, but we didn't need to run anything full time. The old stone fireplace was wonderful in the winter chill, and eventually Gaz even hooked up an old evaporative air conditioner that a friend gave us, so we had air conditioning in summer, which we desperately needed, because when it was fifty Celsius outside, it was about six hundred Celsius inside and I was developing the first real signs of menopause ("Gosh it's hot. No, it's cold. Now I'm going to kill you with this frying pan").

I could write a whole book just about Bush Camp. One of the things I enjoyed most was that we had no actual address, quickly becoming known to locals as "Gaz 'n' Anna's camp" and easily located by our mates who know Meeka like the back of their hand. It was a problem for others though, especially companies wanting to deliver our online-ordered goods. "We don't deliver to post office boxes, we need a street address to give to the freight run driver."

I would try to explain, but it was no use, and eventually I would give them these directions: "OK, tell your driver to take the Wiluna turnoff north of town, then keep going until they pass the dead kangaroo, and start looking for a dirt track on the left. Take the track and keep going past the dead cow, you'll see our tree house on the left. Look out for Red Dog."

There would be a silence at the other end of the line. "Look, it's a small town," I'd say. "Just write Anna the Lady Who Drives Around On The Scooter With the Dog Wearing Goggles on it and leave it at the pub, it will get to me." My friend Fran once addressed a letter to "The Crazy Canadian Lady In The Red Bus, Meekatharra Western Australia The Outback" and it reached me with no problems.

Explaining our address and lifestyle to city folks was an ongoing challenge, as we discovered when we visited Melbourne briefly to meet each other's friends and families. "This is Grandpa, and Grandpa's girlfriend," explained Gary's adult kids to the toddler grandchildren. "Grandpa lives in a shed." The six-year-old looked at us blankly. "Is that where your teeth are, Grandpa?" he asked.

We revelled in Gary's brother & sister-in-law's bathroom for a week. They were very kind and understanding; it must have been like hosting primitive savages. "Gaz! They have COLD WATER!" I rejoiced. Back at bush camp, the cold water was, in the month of January, so hot you couldn't stand under it - we had to set up an inflatable pool in the living room, fill it with hot water from the cold tap, then let it sit overnight under the air conditioner to cool down (I'm not making this up). It was the height of luxury, in Melbourne, to make a cup of coffee without having to gather wood, fight off snakes and carry a blackened kettle across the room with a pair of pliers.

Another time, a young fellow called Chris from the ABC Open television program came into Meeka, looking for some "characters" to interview for a 5-minute TV spot. "Go see Gaz 'n' Anna," someone told him. I raced home in a panic. "Gaz! Put your teeth in! We're going to be on the telly!" It was like the Beverly Hillbillies. We scrubbed up as best we could, and welcomed young Chris into the eclectic disarray of our bush home, filled with "treasures" from the tip, plus motorcycle parts, dogs, furniture made out of mining pallets, and "the snake, but it doesn't usually come out unless it's quiet, and mind you put your shoes on when you go to the loo".

You can find Chris's program on the ABC Open website; it's called "We Don't Need To Catch Up". It features Gary's teeth sitting on the table where we forgot he'd put them as we talked. Gary's brother Robert was kind enough to ring up and let him know. "You idiot," he said. But it was a charming piece which definitely captured the contrast of our crazy city lives and the happiness we feel here under the stars and the big outback sky.

Chris loved Bush Camp so much he didn't want to leave, and instead of staying at the motel found himself happily asleep in one of our spare guest sheds ("there may be lizards, but they're harmless" we assured him) and marvelling at the life we'd accidentally made for ourselves.

And he was right. Gary had built me a tree house at my request, and we spent many hours up there watching the sunsets, the spectacular wet season storms crossing the vast hot land, and the many native birds that came to drink at our pond. We had no microwave, it took an hour to heat up the shower water with the fire under the donkey boiler, there were noises in the night and surprise critters in the outdoor bathroom, it was challenging, grubby, smoky and hard work, but above all, it was good for the soul - and isn't that what home should be?

Meeka nomics

When I first moved to Meeka, I was horrified to discover that the nearest Bunnings was over 500 kilometres away. Like many city folk, I couldn't imagine a world where you can't wander into the vast aisles of a Bunnings store to buy a 2-metre extension lead and come out dazed and delirious with a $5000 pergola kit that's bigger than your actual yard and then your partner is angry and you have to take it back. How would I survive?

But as I soon discovered, set amongst vivid red rocks and stunning outback vistas, there is a place far more wondrous and rewarding than any Bunnings: the Meeka tip. A cornucopia of treasures for those with a resourceful mind and a strong stomach, the local tip changed my life, introducing me to the complex and entertaining world of bush economics, a realm of wild ideas, ingenious inventions and more unfinished projects than you could poke a discarded drill core at. It's also a vibrant social hub, especially on a Saturday morning - if you're new in town, it's a great place to meet the locals and catch up on gossip while eyeing off the potential gems lurking in the back of each other's utes, or sharing finds as you fossick through the pungent, thigh-deep reefs of Emu Bitter cans. That three-legged chair could be restored with a bit of whittling, glueing and painting - and look, here's half of an industrial freezer! We could use it for...something! And what about this perfectly good sofa? We can scrape the dead cat off and it'll be just like new!

Gary knows that there's nothing like a good ol' Saturday tip run to impress a lady, and we spent many happy hours of our early dating days there together, exchanging limpid looks of love from behind the six-inch layer of flies on our faces, then sharing a frisky wire brush detox scrubdown under the high pressure truck wash hose. It didn't take long before we had a superb pile of tip finds and were ready to venture into the Meeka tradition of bartering.

Recycling reaches dizzy heights in Meeka. For example, if you need a gas oven, you just put an ad up at Farmer Jack's (the town supermarket). Then Baz will pop round and say he thinks his old oven is in the shed at Grunter's ex-wife's place which he was going to give to Grunter in exchange for Grunter's dad's old .222 which he didn't want anymore, but then Grunter's missus ran off with that truck driver and the police confiscated the .222 after the shooting incident and Baz doesn't think Grunter will be coming back any time soon so you might as well have the gas oven if you can give one of your old quad bike frames to Rocky who's got a set of axles that Baz needs to fix up the trailer he got from Waz in exchange for Waz fixing up Baz's ex-wife's bloke's Nissan and if you see him tell the bastard he owes me a carton for that gen-set I borrowed off Stevo when I helped him fix Shazza's ute so she could go pick up those pigs she got off Ken.

But it's not always so simple - because not only does the tip breed flies, it also breeds Ideas. "Let's build a wind turbine out of this old diff!" "Yeah! And if we hook it up to this old fuel drum we could make an off-grid washing machine!" "What about these buckets of old chip oil? We could make our own bio-fuel! And I'll save up lots of old jars and make preserves, and you can make a grindstone from that old cistern for our wheat, just like in the olden days!"

We soon realised, however, that in ye oldenne dayyes, Mr. and Mrs. Bush Hovel weren't watching 17 episodes a day of Lost or lying around drunk throwing frogs into the bush and laughing mindlessly at each other's pool farts. Becoming self-sufficient make-do bush dwellers was going to require some tough lifestyle changes, such as getting up before noon. I set my alarm for the ungodly hour of eight a.m. and, after a few cups of coffee, a swim, some light reading and a lie down, I was ready to get stuck into some hard yakka the next day.

I'd already had a childhood brush with self-sufficient living, when my parents decided to embrace the 1970's by purchasing a hobby farm, wearing peasant shirts and subscribing to Mother Earth News, an experiment which basically led to a lot of home-made wine, wild student parties and Theodore the goat eating mum's "special herb plant" and leaping into the swimming pool. There would be no such shenanigans at our place - I was determined to make an effort, at least until lunch time.

I decided to start with some simple, old-school home economies and make my own laundry detergent from basic supermarket products. It was surprisingly easy and cheap, and even got some of the dirt out of our clothes. Inspired, I thought, well, why not make our own hand soaps and cleaning aids? I got on the internet, which always leads to trouble.

It seemed easy enough at first - a few basic ingredients from the garden and the grocery shelf - but then of course to make them all stick together you need to go to some hippy organic gender-free eco-store in Sydney and buy a tiny vial of rare vego-organic beetle spit scraped once every hundred years from endangered leaves by small, stunted Peruvian child slaves, resulting in the cost of your home-made hand soaps coming to about $567 each and smelling like damp alpaca.

But I wasn't ready to give up yet. Surely in ye olden days of yore Mrs. Mud Humpy wasn't relying on gluten-free Madagascan lemur oil to make her household cleaning products? Of course not, she just waited until old Dobbin kicked the bucket and boiled him down in the copper to render him into a handy all-purpose tallow. Simple! Now all I needed was a dead horse.

As luck would have it, we have a dead horse just a short distance away, but as I pondered his single hoof poking out from the ground where the dogs and the bungarras have been nibbling on it, I felt that cooking down some poor bloke's faithful old barrel-racing mate would probably cross some centuries-old line of bush etiquette and perhaps create some awkward moments at the pub. Also, it was 48 degrees in the shade, and I suspected that Gary wouldn't want to come home to find me retching helplessly next to a stinking vat of liquefying horse remains ("I'll have dinner ready soon"), and I was pretty sure that boiling down a decaying horse would not result in a "lemony fresh" fragrance.

Anyway, we've decided to keep things simple, because let's face it, we don't really want to spend 37 hours a day labouring in our itchy hand-spun dog-hair trousers, scraping bungarra hides in the burning noonday sun or whittling Landcruiser clutch parts out of discarded mine pallets as we listen to the weevils in our home-grown baked beans exploding like popcorn in the recycled bio-fuel chip fat, washing ourselves with a rag on a stick because we used all the rainwater to make raw camp whiskey. So we're just going to grow a few vegies and Gary is going to set up some solar panels, except I think I may have accidentally traded Gary for an old Lister gen-set and a set of 16-ply tyres in a confusing arrangement involving Tony, Steve, a clawfoot bathtub, Stickman, a dog? and one of the Thundelarra utes, so if one of you has ended up with Gary, please bring him home. I'll pay cash.

my Fiend the wind

Gary and I decided that we would get a simple off-grid wind and solar kit for our bush camp home. As the official googler, it was my job to do the research and work out what to buy. Sun, panels, turbine, batteries - how hard could it be? With Gaz balancing precariously on our tin roof with the antenna from the bus ("THAT'S PERFECT, DON'T MOVE!"), I hopped on to the internet.

Three weeks later my sanity was teetering on the abyss from downloading sine wave charts, amp-wattage calculator tools and wading through dense sales gibberish from companies with names like "Too Many Details R Us Hybrid Incomprehensible Solar Solutions" and "Whatever You Need Will Cost Way More Than You Could Possibly Imagine Ha Ha Ha Eco-Solar Pirates Inc". Delirious with confusion, I decided to call some friendly experts for help. Here's how it went:

Me:
Hi, I'm calling about your off-grid solar kit.

Mr. Sales Guy:
We have a great off-grid kit starting at $150,000, but that doesn't include an amp-modulated pro sine-wave dumpload pre-charge regulator, and of

course our team of technicians will need to come out and assess whether you have the sufficient 1.7 square kilometres of mountable prestressed roof area for the 432 panels, depending on whether you go with the monocrystalline multi-flex high-res hurricane resistor model or the PV sola-amp pro nutech plasma combo packs, which of course need the optional torque-volt meter multi-synchro transformer. It's a great beginner's pack.

Me:
I think we'll just stick to sitting in the dark and eating raw mice, thank you.

. . . .

Me:
Hi, I'd like some help choosing a small off grid solar system.

Oz-E Solar:
Hello! My name Weewee! I help you for most quality productives! You want Hello Kitty so-rar system, we got a rot, you give me credit card number now!

Me:
Goodbye Weewee.

. . . .

Me:
Hi, we're looking for a solar and wind kit for a small household.

Baz:
Yer just need the 3 kilowatt turbine, controller and inverter for about five grand all up. Where are yer?

Me:
Meekatharra. It's --

Baz:
I know where it is, I'll drive it all up to yers when I'm done me seedin'. What batteries yer usin?

Me:
Oh, that sounds great. Well, what batteries should we get?

Baz:
Well that depends, see if yer go with 6 volt pro packs yer need about 48 of em they're not cheap, but if yer usin' more than 300 amp hours per kilobyte you shouldn't get truck batteries, or just go 24 volt but it'll catch fire. Yer'd have to wire the lot in parallel but then yer got a problem with how much wirin' yer got to get, it's not cheap. What regulator yer usin? If it's not 18 volt it'll catch fire.

Me:
I'll call you back later, after I finish self-mutilating.

So that's how we decided to just build a bloody wind turbine ourselves out of old car parts and things from the tip. We'll be sure to keep the fire extinguisher handy.

Western Australia - where men are men and ... Ewww

My city girlfriends are keen watchers of "The Farmer Wants A Wife" (or, as we call it, "Who The Hell Would Want To Be A Farmer??") and were curious about the single bloke situation in Western Australia, so I prepared this handy guide for any urban gals thinking of making the move. You could get lucky, like me, and find yourself a Gary Hammer, a fine specimen of outback blokeness, easily fed on sausages and eggs, and darn handy with his toolkit. But before you tell all your city gal-pals to start packin' their bags and heading out on the Great Western Man Hunt, here are a few tips I've gleaned from actual personal experience:

First, you may need to drop your standards somewhat. In fact, I would recommend not bringing any standards at all. Outback blokes are worth their weight in gold, but you'll need to assess your priorities, or as Dr. Phil likes to call them, "deal breakers". Are teeth important to you? What about underwear? West Australian men don't have underwear, and yours will only suffer the indignities attendant on the startling courtship rituals of the outback. A few pairs of comfy cottontails would be fine as long as you don't mind rescuing them from the diesel rag bin from time to time (behind the genny shed, next to the spare fuel lines).

Bring plenty of sunblock, but don't offer it to a bloke; this will only lead to a derisive snort of amusement, a terse shake of the head, and, some years later, irreparable skin cancer. Any supplies you bring will be immediately ransacked, but generally outback blokes are gentlemen and once they've used your Gillete Lady razors to shave off the feral pig carcass in the ute, they will return it promptly to your bathroom kit.

Do some muscle-building exercises, as you will need strong arms for carrying the minimum requirement of 3 cases of beer per man/hour - and none of that schmancy woofter beer either, it needs to be a good, solid full-strength fightin' beer. If he's "on the piss" with his "mates", you may want to consider a separate sleeping arrangement for the night, such as Perth.

So, how do you go about meeting an outback bloke? Unlike the subtle confusions of city romance, here all you need to do is stand still for a minute or two (carry a stick). If you are a blonde Danish backpacker, run for your life.

Here are some typical opening lines to help you know when a bloke is indicating a romantic interest: "Youse wanna come to me room? Oi've got beer." "There's space in the dog box if you don't mind it standing up", and "I'm hammered but I reckon youse could still hang a wet towel on it love".

Refreshingly, jealousy is rarely an issue. If he was to spot you in the grubby embrace of one of his mates outside a roadhouse donger, he would simply stride past with a quick "Gidday Baz mate ow yer goin orright". His mate would reply "Yer no worries mate didja get that diesel outa the ute orright mate?", by which time he will have finished and you can continue on your way to the shower block (carry a sharp tyre iron).

You'll know things are getting serious if he asks you to come roo shootin' with him on Friday night or jots your phone number down on the back of one of his restraining orders. A truly lovesick bloke will suffer the jocular abuse of his mates in all directions for fifty kilometres in order to put on a shirt without holes in it from the floor of the shed before taking you to the roadhouse for "some effin' grouse fried chook mate". He will also make an effort to observe some of the finer points of dating etiquette, such as remembering your name.

Remember that the poor fellow hasn't seen a non-angry woman for approximately six months, so he'll need to bolster his courage with astonishing amounts of beer - but don't worry, his internal organs have pretty much shut down from living on alcohol and chiko rolls, so it won't affect his ability to brag about his prowess. If you feel the need for tender, wordless companionship, a sharp blow to the back of his head with a handy spanner should do the trick (but wait until he's fixed the shower block pump first). A home-cooked meal is always welcome, but remember to measure your quantities in "whole animal"; anything found recently dead at the side of the road will suffice if a supermarket isn't handy. Avoid vegetables - they will only confuse and anger him.

If you feel like complaining at the oily paw marks on your favorite fancy bra (what were you thinking?), just remember that those same paws have been busy fixing the genny, gutting a pig for dinner and pumping out the septic because you were too princessy to wee behind the shed. Of course your frillies will never be the same and that morning-after roo 'n' beer breath could knock out a horse, but would you rather listen to Mr. Mocha Latte waffle on about how he's not ready for a relationship as he busily texts his internet dates about "catching up for a drink sometime LOL"?

Despite all this, there are some downsides, so be prepared. You don't want to be having second thoughts when it's fifty-five degrees and you're trapped in a dogbox watching Shark Safari III for the two thousandth time while making ammo casings next to someone whose toiletry kit consists of a rusty fish knife and a bar of soap that looks suspiciously like an old urinal cube. But I won't hold you up any longer - I can tell you're keen to get packing.

domestic blisters

My friends back east think my life is wildly romantic, living in the rugged outback with a tall, handsome fire brigade captain, but I've had to tell them that it's not all flaming sunsets and sweaty hose-handling. Gary has had to suffer stoically as I put aside my nail polish and single-gal city ways in order to confront the gruelling hardships of the bush, such as cooking.

We don't cook in the city - we have iPhones apps instead - so when Gary and I shacked up, my culinary skills were pretty much limited to staring blankly into the fridge, then wishing I still had a personal assistant so that I could send them to the roadhouse for a pie.

I decided I would start my domestic journey with sandwich making, which is how I discovered that Gary, despite many happy years on a simple bachelor diet of Jatz crackers, turned into Gordon Ramsay when it came to me making his smoko. "These cheese slices are too thick! Make them thinner! That's too thin! And there's too much butter! Where's the tomato sauce?" Then he wanted me to label each sandwich wrapper so he knew what was in them. "Okay," I said sweetly, getting out the texta. He's gotten used to finding things in his smoko labelled "Diced Squid" and "Enraged Bear Parts".

But perhaps the biggest challenge has been sharing a home. As most of us know, other people have strange, intolerable habits, wantonly violating the toothpaste tube, bizarrely putting the cling wrap in the second drawer, and making you almost homicidally annoyed with their insane, unreasonable demands such as "Where's the tin opener?" and "Have you seen my keys?". But as adults, we are forced to cope and adjust, handling these day-to-day challenges with calm maturity, unless of course it's forty-five degrees and there's no air conditioning and you have level 10 menopause and there's an axe handy.

I've had to learn a range of cohabitation skills, such as Shouting From The Back Room, What Is This Doing In The Fridge, and Did You Leave Them In Your Other Pants. The trick is to be patient and forgiving, especially if you are Gary and have to put up with a selectively deaf partner who can't understand basic engine components and would, left to her own devices, allow the chooks to sleep on the bed (next to the baby kangaroo and a sick alpaca).

Naturally this leads us to the horrors of shared sleeping arrangements. As we're all aware, other people selfishly move around and make noises in bed, waking us up in the night with their ghastly internal expulsions and Tourette's-like fidgeting, coughing and moaning until they have to be poked sharply in the kidneys and told to sleep in the other room. Poor Gary! It can't be easy, trying to sleep with a girlfriend whose sleeping habits, according to him, could rival the more violent scenes from the Exorcist.

Of course there are many good things about living with someone, once you accept that they are probably clinically insane and will never develop basic mind-reading skills or stop listening to that godawful rubbish that they call music. There are many tender, intimate moments - a lingering gaze as we engage in hand-to-hand combat over the last of the Aerogard or selflessly exchanging the crippling gastrointestinal disorder that one of us brought home from town. And of course there are the many practical benefits - having a partner at your side certainly helps with things like "Does This Smell All Right To You?", "Gary The Generator's Making A Funny Noise" and "Honey Can You Go Stand Out On The Flats With The

Internet Aerial While I Update My Facebook Page?".

But perhaps the greatest pleasure is living together in a small town - unlike city life, we don't have to "catch up" outside our busy schedules. Work and socialising all blend together through the day as I take Gary's smoko out to him on my bush bike, or pause to shout at each other about genny fuel across the road as he rumbles past in the tipper truck. Forget the roses and chocolates of city romance - my heart says there's nothing better than coming home sweaty and tired from putting out scrub fires together at three in the morning, sharing a cuppa with my bloke in the romantic flickering candlelight, tenderly --- oh, hang on, we don't have candles. Bugger! I forgot to take the chicken out of the fire pit. Do you mind if it's a bit black?

Our trip to the big city

Gary and I steeled ourselves after New Year's and ventured east to the dazzling big city lights of Melbourne to visit family and friends, and, more importantly, McDonalds. It was my first time flying from Meeka, and it was charming to be on the small prop plane filled with people we know. Gaz and I were pleased to see that Lauren and Anne were in charge of opening the wing-side emergency hatch, mostly because we were pretty sure we could overpower them if it came to hand-to-hand combat in the screaming stampede to get out first.

As fire and rescue volunteers, Gaz and I are trained to plan for emergencies, so we alertly memorised which of our Meeka neighbours would make the best eating if we crashed in the desert, and, having recently watched the entire series of "Lost", snatched as many handfuls of complimentary biscuits from the hostess as possible while fashioning rudimentary hunting tools from our coffee cups.

At Perth we headed over to Qantas where helpful airline staff frisked all of us outback travellers for roo-gutting knives, mining detonators, .222 ammo and whatever was left on our credit cards before releasing us in a wild melee for the bookshop, coffee bar and Krispy Kreme donut stand. On the plane, we marvelled at all the fancy new improvements, such as the individual touch-screen DVD players on the back of each seat and the complete lack of room available if, like Gary, you were thoughtless enough to bring your legs on the flight.

We were greeted at Melbourne airport by my friend June, who warned us that the temperature was 35 degrees, so we quickly rugged up and stared goggle-eyed at the sight of traffic lights, other cars on the road, and trees. There wasn't time for sightseeing, though, as we had to keep to our tight visiting schedule of 3.6 minutes per person. Gary's brother and sister in law generously lent us a car, and even let us use their renovated bathroom. It was lovely to use a loo without having to peel frogs off our arses, and to drink tap water that didn't taste like a dingo had died in it.

Our visit was everything we could have asked for - the warmth of familiar, loved faces, remembering funny times, and being welcomed by Gary's family. I never dreamed I would live to see the day I'd be introduced as "Grandpa's Girlfriend", or possibly worse, "Nana Anna"! Gary's new teeth were too uncomfortable for him to wear, so we kept them handy in my purse to be brought out during awkward conversational lulls. "Gary's just about the only bloke in Meeka with nice false teeth like these," we bragged. Everyone marvelled at our descriptions of bush camp life, chasing snakes out of the garden and finding bungarras in the rubbish bin under the roasting outback summer sun. "It sounds like you're having a great time! We're never, ever coming to visit!"

Numb from 1,237 showings of The Slide Show on my laptop ("That's our shed...that's another shot of the shed...here's the shed from another angle..."), we finished off our visiting rounds with a trip to Echuca, where we forced Gary's mum to enjoy a paddle steamer trip ("I think I need to lie down now"), then headed back to the city for final farewells.

My friend Polly kindly drove us to the airport, which took longer than actually driving to Perth because Polly is a bit navigationally challenged. My friend Sally helped me put our baggage through the infernally complicated self check-in machines, and then we went to rescue Gary from airport security.

Gaz had been pulled aside for having a small, cheap multi-function pocket tool in his carry-on bag. They threw it in the bin and we escaped, relieved, because although they found the perfectly harmless pocket tool, they missed the 20 kilograms of military large-gun ammo casings, one of which weighed 9 kilos on its own and took up most of Gary's travel bag (they were de-commissioned souvenirs from Gary's brother which we were taking back for the Mess at Paddy's Flat). I had visions of being confronted at Perth airport with a full police lock-down and only seconds to choke "I love you" to each other while being dragged handcuffed into the waiting divvy vans, then being featured on Border Security.

We made it to Perth without incident, however, apart from severe cramping due to Qantas having reduced the economy seating space by another six inches since our earlier flight. Gary stowed his legs in the overhead luggage compartment and we used our noses to operate the DVD touchscreens. The screaming baby who follows me on every single flight I have ever taken in my life was, predictably, just a few seats away, and I wondered for the thousandth time why they don't just release a heavy-duty sleeping gas into the passenger cabin on all flights and bundle your unconscious body onto the baggage carousel with your luggage at the other end. They'd save heaps on complimentary pretzels.

After all this excitement, our big night at the Perth Grand Medina Hotel was reduced to staring blearily at the TV and cleaning out the mini bar before passing out on the acre-sized hotel bed. After a few hours' sleep, we pulled some clean socks out of the ammo casings, handed over our life savings to pay for the mini bar, and joined the hordes of mine workers at Skippers airline terminal for the flight back to "the ends of the earth". Cam and Monica collected us at the Meeka airport and took us home to be greeted by our overexcited dogs ("You're home! We missed you We ate your shoes!"), the soothing roar of the generator and our 50,000 pet flies.

Our visit to Melbourne knitted many aspects of our lives together - our old city life and our new Meeka life, Gary's past and my past, bringing together family, friends and old memories - and I'm glad we went.

But it also made us realise that even though we've only been here a relatively short time, we're Meeka people now. The city seems to be mainly about shopping and money, texting and traffic; trying to find work and stressing over an ever-increasing burden of debt. Apart from our loved ones, Melbourne held no appeal for us at all. As we explained to our city friends, we have much less than they do in the city, but it means we have so much more. Our lives are richer for the challenge, being part of keeping the town going and seeing each day that what you do makes a difference - it's a feeling of self-worth and pride that can't be bought at the mall. And who needs matching Ikea furniture or a shiny new car when you have pretty little ta-ta lizards waving at you in the bathroom and a flock of jewel-bright budgies filling the blue afternoon sky?

If our families ever do come to visit though, just don't mention the scorpions, and please remember to put your teeth in. You can borrow Gary's if you like - they're in my handbag, next to the ammo.

Orstraya Day Mate

In Canada, our national day is a tidy, well-behaved affair - we pry the icicles off the flag, put a traditional snack of wood chips out for the beavers, decorate the town moose with pine cones and politely exchange frozen salmon treats while mumbling the national anthem, which goes like this:

"O Canada, our something something land, true something mumble, in all our coughcoughmumble. With glowing? snowing? hearts we somethingorother our true north somethinglingly, so stand on guard O Canada, we stand on guard for --- Dad, why do we have to stand on guard? SHHH. YOU'RE SUPPOSED TO BE SINGING NOW. But Dad, why? SHH! smack Oww Daaad !!"

Australia Day, however, is much more fun, because it celebrates our national icons of drinking, inflatable pools, fake flag tattoos and boisterously joining in patriotic songs such as The Angels' "Am I Ever Gonna See Your Face Again?", to which everyone in Australia knows the words from the age of 5 (in comparison to the actual national anthem, which goes "Orstrayans oar let arse ring Joyce for she is young and free, mumble mumble righto time for a smoke").

I had the great privilege of attending the Murchison Downs Homestead Australia Day festivities this year, my first big outback party, and it was just terrific, especially the bits that happened before my 9th beer (I know, I'm sorry, I'm trying to increase my beer capacity but it takes time to kill your liver off so that it no longer poses a barrier to the rigours of

Meeka consumption levels).

I was amazed at the generosity and hard work of the Howdens and caretakers Lindsay and Ben in providing us all with delicious home made food, and it was great to see how so many people contributed with minibike rides for the kids, decorations, comfy lawn mattresses to pass out on, pool fun and of course entertainment from "the band", featuring my handsome personal emu-identifier ("that's Harold, and that one's Betty"), Gary Hammer, who proved he can not only play harmonica but can also line dance at the same time. Is there no limit to his talents?

My highlights of the day were a ponytrap ride with Lindsay and little Chutney, who was fetchingly decked out in a braided mane and Australian flags, seeing all the wonderfully battered old hats on the heads of local station folk, helping dollop cream on to Lindsay's mini pavlovas, and snuggling up to Meacho on his fabulous new double camp sofa (available at Farmer Jack's, get yours quick).

It was also impressive to see Lauren (Loz) Howden setting out lamingtons and pavlova in her traditional outfit of shorts, neat country shirt, bush hat, blunny boots and pearls - every time I see Loz, I feel envious and harbour dreams of being a jillaroo, dusty and sweaty but keeping up standards in an understated but verrrry classy set of pearl earrings. No one can carry this off like a dinky-di Aussie outback woman - Loz could bring down and hog-tie a two thousand kilo enraged bull in foot-deep pindan dust and mud and still come out looking perfectly ready to host a Country Women's Association fundraiser. I, on the other hand, can spend hours getting myself ready and still look like I was hastily dressed by an angry, underpaid carer.

Anyway, another big highlight was that I managed not to fall into the pool with a beer in my hand, although there was a slightly unladylike incident in some bushes as I tried to remember where the loo was in the dark while wearing (why?) platform sandals. Thankfully I did not partake of The Punch, which was served in satanically colourful cocktail glasses the size of buckets and goes some way to explaining why certain people (not naming any names here, Cath Evans!) might not have been at their 100%

best the next day at the post office. Ahem.

And what a smorgasbord of musical talent we feasted on! I loved Clarrie's moving and beautifully written self-composed bush songs, with him looking the part in his bush hat, stubbies and blunnies, and who could forget Tom and Gary's epic improvised blues performance of "Smoky Train"? If you were busy scoffing lamingtons at the time, it went like this:

"Smoky train......goin' on down the line.....smoky traaain .... goin' on down the liiiine......whoo! smoky train....yeah...smoky, smoky train...goin' on...dowwwwn the line...."

After about half an hour, ol' smoky train had gone down the line, over the hill and was about to start comin' on down the line again but Tom & Gaz suddenly realised they needed more alcohol, which was lucky for them because a few of us were thinking about how to pull up the tracks on ol' smoky train, possibly with an esky lid and any other handy blunt instruments. "What kinda train didja say that was?" I asked as they retired, demonstrating my excellent Beer Humour skills.

With Eric and his musical genius holding it all together, the band provided us with much hilarity and opportunities for sing-alongs, some of which we managed to hear over the volume of the extremely keen rogue lead guitarist. Adam Howden unleashed his inner rock star, and our local and Irish backpacker gals made a valiant rescue attempt on the band's startling assault on "Wonderwall", after which we all needed a bit more beer and a second visit to the dessert table. In true outback style, it wasn't about being perfect, but just having a go and having a laugh with mates, and once again we were reminded that we have some very talented musos in our midst. I am so proud of Gary for coming out of the harmonica closet this year and having the guts to play in front of an audience!

I think most of us would agree that the absolute highlight of the night was SJ, our recent Korean arrival - this is a massive sideline story, but SJ arrived in Meeka with his two travelling companions when their GPS led them off into the bush towards Wiluna, where they rolled their van. Locals took them back to Meeka, got them jobs, moved them into my house with my tenant at the time, Crazy Dave, who, in a fit of community spirit, made them join the State Emergency Services' search for the body of a missing prospector, and when they got back they discovered that another body had been dumped against my back fence after a terrible domestic dispute and the forensic police from Perth had sealed off the back yard as a crime scene - this is all true - and I was waiting out the front of the house to discuss a sale price on the house with Dave, wondering how having a murder victim lying against the back fence was going to affect the property value, and also thinking that the Koreans would be madly texting their friends and family back home with startling travel information: "When in Austraya, traditional all must help in the looking for dead people, of which being there are many." I wondered when it would turn up on Trip Advisor.

OK, so there in front of a mob of drunken Aussie yahoos yelling like barbarians was SJ, playing in the band - and he not only impressed us with a poppin' good drum solo, but blew us all away when he got up to sing his own song in Korean and English.

"I am very nervous! I am going to sing in Korean! Sorry!"

"Nah, go on mate, you'll be right!" came the boozy cry from the crowd. We were all beerily cheering him on, and he started off a little hesitantly. Coming from the polite, restrained Asian world, it must have been like facing of a mob of wild, roaring Vikings.

WELL. He soon had us rapt and astonished as he gave us a professional, moving, passionate performance of his song "Don't Give Up", leading the band with his dexterous guitar work and abandoning himself to the power of his music, taking us all with him and leaving us gobsmacked. I don't know about anyone else, but I felt quite emotional and teary, watching this brave young bloke share his music and his heart with us. We all stood up and applauded, welcoming this foreign visitor into the fold - it was like a Meekatharra citizenship ceremony!

Australia Day means many things to many people - we think of the past, of the men and women who gave their lives in our country's name, and those who bravely serve now in so many places overseas. We think of the hardship of early colonial days and the grief that was brought to the aboriginal inhabitants, the sorrow of distant and recent pasts for those who were here and those who came later, and we argue and wonder about who's true blue and who should be allowed in.

But, like being in Meeka, I think that being Australian is what you make of it - it doesn't matter if you were born here or got here last week; what matters is who you are, what you share, and "having a go". Sure, the pavs, beer and flags are all a wonderful part of the celebration, but it was the way our town welcomed a young Korean singing and playing guitar under an outback moon which gave me a rare and delightful insight into what Australia Day can be about. Good on ya, Meeka!

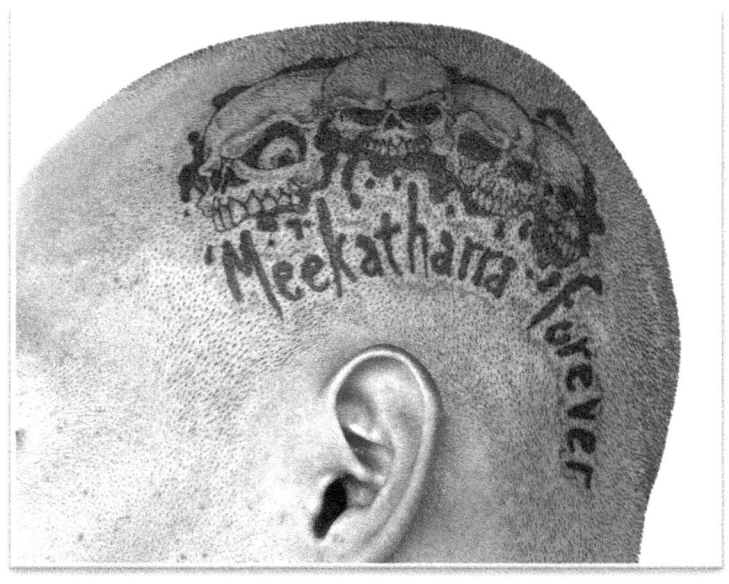

SJ loved Meekatharra so much that he got this tattooed on his head. He left Meeka to continue his travels, but we're pretty sure he'll be back.

in the ear of the beholder

One of the things I love about Meeka are the free visiting medical services. Sure, sometimes it's a gaggle of nervous grad students whose hands shake with performance anxiety as they try to read the instruction manual and perform delicate surgical repairs on your exposed nerve endings at the same time, standing on a stool because they're only 12 years old or something and can't reach the operating table yet, but they do a great job and it's certainly a step up from the home first aid kit (a machete and a gun).

This month's visiting specialist was the optometrist, which was exciting because Gaz and I are slowly going blind from living with dim 12 volt lighting and storing our reading glasses under the 50-metre tape measure, angle grinder and roofing nails that I typically carry in my handbag (I like to be prepared).

The optical team were a very nice Indian couple from Perth with fancy Oxford accents (I think they may have been practising in the car on the way up). Like most of our visiting medical professionals, they were not only highly skilled and efficient, but also extraordinarily patient and polite, wearing startlingly clean, ironed clothes - you could tell straightaway they weren't from around here. Feeling soiled and barbaric, I made a pathetic effort to hide my muddy, unshaven legs by pulling my work socks as high as the decayed elastic would allow, while Gary rummaged through my handbag for his teeth.

Gaz is still trying to get used to his handsome new teeth - we generally reserve them for emergency social situations (we're fond of telling our city friends that they're the Town Teeth and it's our week to have them). The problem is that they are attached to a dental plate the size of a roadhouse pie, which makes Gaz gag and causes his listeners to back away in alarm, then I have to try and translate, which isn't easy because my hearing isn't so good because I refused to listen to my mum when she shouted at me in my room when I was thirteen IF YOU KEEP LISTENING TO THAT GODAWFUL MUSIC AT THAT VOLUME YOUNG LADY YOU'LL GO DEAF and she was right.

Anyway, that's all a very longwinded preamble to why the divinely patient optometrists will be reincarnated as gods, because this is what they had to put up with:

Gary: Dush thesshe look shtrigit?
Me: What?
Gary: Deef! Deef shtrigit!
Me: They look great, just don't talk.
Nurse: Ms. Johnson, if you would kindly take a seat here the eye doctor will see you now.
Me: Sorry, what was that?
Nurse: THE DOCTOR WILL SEE YOU NOW PLEASE.
Gary: Shegh's uhg bit deaguf!
Nurse: I beg your pardon?
Me: What?
Doc: Ms. Johnson, will you be wanting combination frames or would you prefer a pair?
Me: Panther repair?

We left the poor optometrists to wrestle with half a dozen small children who were excitedly eating the chairs and headed back into the rain and mud with our glasses prescriptions. We are still recovering from the credit-card ravaging effects of last month, when our poor little cattle dog, who is also coincidentally deaf (try to keep up here) broke her leg, so our prescriptions are nailed to the wall in the shed for later, by which time our eyesight will be so poor that we won't be able to see them anymore and will have to hope that the non-deaf dogs can lead us to safety, or the fridge.

loose elastic and a nice lie down

I turned fifty this year. As one of my friend's children said, "You are very, very Old," as if I was a tortoise, or a museum exhibit. I could hear the David Attenborough commentary: "This ancient specimen of Johnson creaks and shambles on its determined trek towards the refrigerator, where its age-raddled brain struggles to recall just what it wanted inside... abandoning this plan, it sags slowly to the ground, resting its decrepit legs for a few hours before trying again."

Working in aged care, I've been fortunate in getting much helpful advice from older people, who, as we know, are Wise. "If I was your age young lady I wouldn't get married or work or anything, I'd put on a red dress and run around town having a good time, bloody oath I would" and "If I'd shot my husband when I met him, I'd be out of jail now."

By following this sort of advice, I got to where I am today - living in a scorpion-infested shed in the desert with my handsome personal harmonica player, Gary Hammer, and a resident toilet bat. I could so easily have been trapped in a lovely renovated house with central heating, a car with all its window-winders working, cafés and malls just down the street, and an ulcer the size of that gut-bursting thing from Alien thriving on the stress from my high-end executive job.

Growing older is all about attitude. You're either a "glass half empty" or a "glass half full" person, or, in my case, a person who says "Where did I put that glass? Did I have a drink going already? Has anyone seen where I left my tablets?" This happens because as you get older, your body stops making fresh brain cells and the few (3) brain cells that said No To Drugs in your youth are now paralysed with hundreds of PIN numbers, Secret Questions and your Facebook log-in passwords.

As a kid, your priorities are things like mud fights, throwing spiders at your friend's sister and hoping that mum won't find out that you and your brothers encouraged the horse into the kitchen. But as you get older, you find yourself making Sensible Decisions, such as having a nap instead of drinking yourself paralytic & topless at biker bars, and buying large bulk-pack underpants with loose, comfortable elastic.

Proper grownups do budgeting and Putting Something Away For The Future. Gaz and I have been giving this a go, but this is difficult when you're the kind of people who would buy a surplus helicopter on eBay for no reason or, as we did last month, build a tree house instead of going to work.

Anyway, budgeting only reveals that you will never, ever come close to saving up the 15 million dollars that the financial boffins reckon you will need for retirement, so you might as well just have fun while hoping that one of the kids becomes the next Bill Gates and buys you a luxury aged-care spa-castle island.

Having reached the half-century mark, I feel extraordinarily lucky - yes, my knees are stuffed, my internal organs make startling noises and doctors who look like they're 17 years old want to stick various oscopies up my nether regions, but for me, growing older means that you Know Stuff, like how to frighten 19-year-old Telstra call centre youths or, finally, realising that drinking a full bottle of straight scotch will only make you beg to be euthanased the next morning, and of course appreciating that the benefits of blowing an entire paycheque on a Glow In The Dark Inflatable Nativity Scene Complete With Talking Camel far outweigh the inconvenience of have to eat lentils and roast chihuahua for a month.

You'll have to excuse me now - it's time for another attempt on the fridge to make Gary some lovely bark and grass sandwiches. I might just have a quick lie down first. Do you mind checking the horse tallow boiler every half hour? It might overflow, and it's a bugger getting the smell out of the floorboards.

Would you like my brain with that?

Alert Dust readers may have noticed that I recently started working at the roadhouse. Based on my earlier roadhouse experience of working at the Overlander, where the only job qualification was to be sober enough to put your shoes on the correct feet (your own), I figured it would be a reasonably easy sort of job, requiring perhaps half an hour of learning to use the touch-screen and where to locate the diesel drive-off shotgun.

As I quickly discovered however, working at the Meeka roadhouse is very challenging. First of all, not only do you have to turn up for work not drunk, you also have to complete something like 79 online training modules, memorising pie temperatures, fuel types and how to deal with a range of alarming emergency situations such as imminent LPG explosions and armed teenage gangs on crack.

At the Overlander, all we had to worry about were arse-grabbing bus drivers, lonely truckies lurking out the back with handfuls of cash ("I promise I won't take long love and youse can get back to yer cleanin'") and Craig, who was convinced that we were being aerial-sprayed by sinister government biochemical aircraft every Thursday afternoon. But I plowed through the training modules, making a note that, disappointingly, it is not workplace policy to wrestle a gun-wielding robber to the floor, seizing his Glock and jamming it against his balaclava-clad head while screaming for everyone to *Get Down!*, and finally Judy said it was time to go and learn The Console.

The Console is a brilliant, terrifying beast - a touch-screen system that can simultaneously turn pumps on, ring up purchases, calculate discounts and launch interstellar NASA spacecraft. It sounds easy, doesn't it? Ha ha. There should be an annual Checkout Chick National Day Of Honour, because people come in with requests such as "Can I have 7 packs of Winfield Red no JustSmokes Blue no umm hang on I'll just go ask Mum but can I pay for the sausage roll separate from the Freddo's and still get the discount if I use half of this fuel voucher and put the FlyBuys on it later if we buy the 2 for 1 deal on Dad's card and pay for the rest of it with this card from The Obscure Regional Bank Of The People's Republic Of East Lichtenstein?"

At the same time, you also need to keep feeding hundreds of pies into the oven, stock up the milk and bread, pry sugar-crazed children away from the hot chocolate dispenser, clean the showers, sift out the bottle caps and twelve-rupee pieces from the Armenian tourist trying to pay for 103 dollars' worth of diesel with coins, give directions to confused Swedish backpackers who think they're at Mount Augustus (which is 450 km away, and, astonishingly, looks like a MOUNTAIN, you MORONS) then go and rescue the lady who's locked herself in toilet 3 before sprinting outside to hurl yourself on the bonnet of the ute trying to do a drive-off from the diesel pump. By the end of your shift you can't remember your own name and the buttons on the touch screen seem to say things like "Xplrg", "Glarp" and "Wheee!".

The training course videos didn't prepare me for actual Meeka situations. For a start, we are required to communicate without swearing, which of course means that most locals are unable to understand us. There's also Truck Driver Communications. "Yer how long ave them mermaids been ere love?" "Who? What?" "Them scalies out front." "Eh?" "Ferget it, just something something mumble."

So I've started my own set of Meeka Customer Training Instructions. For example, if my handsome personal solar panel installer, Gary Hammer, comes in during his smoko break and tries to buy girlie magazines, say sternly, "Put that back! I'm not working my fingers to the bone just so you can blow our joint savings on cheesy pictures of things you can see for free at home, and while you're here go get milk and bread and don't forget to see Norm about that generator!" Also, make sure Gaz buys more pies and snacks so I don't have to cook anything for dinner later, and if Richard comes in later and tries to buy the same magazines, make sure he fills out the "I Promise I'm Not Buying These For Gary" form.

Despite these innovative ideas, I still have much to learn, as evidenced by my Day Of Hell. Wildly overconfident in my trainee skills, Tom and Judy, who deserve a medal for working day & night while remaining sane and cheerful, went out to do some chores and get their annual dose of half an hour of sunlight. As soon as they left, 2700 customers came in and began eating all the pies, cleaning out the milk supply and generally making a nuisance of themselves by buying things and asking questions. But I kept my training in mind, stayed calm, and it was all going well. Then Wobbly Old Man came in.

His crime: to be old, wobbly and a little bit slow, a sin in our busy tap-swipe-don't-forget-my-flybuys-points-get-me-on-the-road-quick world. As he pecked in shaky confusion at the PIN pad and I tried to help with my sum total knowledge of Not A Lot, we managed, with grimly determined teamwork, to bring the entire system to a halt. The Console went blank, then began displaying messages such as "Customer Purchase Options Are Not Available At This Time" and "System Meltdown - Auto Self Destruct Sequence Will Commence In 10 Seconds". I tapped hopelessly at the screen, making panicked field mouse noises. "Have I done something wrong?" asked Wobbly Old Man in a small, helpless voice.

Soon the bowsers were four deep with caravans, road trains were filling the yard, dozens of children were savaging the lolly rack, truckies were fighting like wolves over the last of the pies, an entire family was either playing rugby or slaughtering wild pigs in toilet 4, and the phone was ringing with people asking things like "We being from Lithuania not having wise of road will you be having thinks of wasteland conditioner eastwest of

Mountain Maggenett mostly similar to caravan?"

Feeling my brain begin to creak, I experienced a flash of hope - perhaps my mind would simply snap and I could run screaming down the middle of the road, permanently insane and absolved of all responsibility, spending the rest of my days slumped in a corner of our shed with Gary spooning vitamised mush into my happily slack, drooling mouth. But I knew it would be wrong - I'd be letting Tom & Judy down, and worse, I would forfeit my Bronze Achievement Star. I looked over the counter at the growing queue, which now reached halfway down Main Street. They were staring. They were all staring.

I rang Mandy, who is conveniently kept locked up in the staff donger out the back for such emergencies, and she deftly tapped away at the console like Scotty on Star Trek, overriding its core brain and re-igniting the main engine's dilithium crystals; with bated breath, we watched the Final Self Destruct Sequence clock stop at 0:001, then the system rebooted. Smiley face!

Wobbly Old Man creaked carefully back to his vehicle to negotiate his slow and cautious way along our road-train infested highway; he seemed a little shell-shocked and I felt sorry for him. I also wanted to ring ahead to Capricorn to warn them of his impending arrival ("Don't let him use the PIN pad!!") but I was surrounded by a chaos of weeping children, mums shouting PUTTHATBACK, grey nomads trying to remember who'd used which pump and someone chasing an excited terrier past the weary people camping in the biscuit aisle.

It was the truckies, along with Mandy and Kath, god bless them, who restored order. One bloke mopped out the toilet horror in cubicle 4, a couple of others refilled the coffee machine, and another bloke stood near the console saying "You'll be right love, just take it step by step" in a soothing, hypnotic tone until I started breathing again and my eyes rolled back into their normal position. Kath, who is one of our wonderful and unflappable staff workers, took over with her Mum-like, legendary efficiency while I went to curl up in the foetal position behind the Coke delivery pallet.

It was awful, but it was great too - people helped, and no one tried to drive off or claw their way over the counter in a frustrated rage to beat me to death with their discount milk. Even more amazingly, Judy and Tom didn't sack me, even though Jude will probably be sorting out that day's paperwork for the next 34 years.

We continue to have busy days and I still feel nervous, but now when I have a customer who's confused or slow I remind myself that we all deserve some patience and help as we cope with a hurried, quick-snack fly-buy world, our pockets slowly filling with the stray bottle caps, strange coins and flotsam of our varied lives as we make our wobbly way through life, the road that all of us share.

stay calm and grab the emergency sock

Gary, being highly protective, has often given me dire warnings about scorpions, insisting that the smaller they are, the more poisonous their bite, with the smaller species being able to kill you, then telling me horror stories about giant scorpions in the Amdel sheds that will still try to have a go at you even after being put in a jar of metho for three days. So naturally when I got stung on the foot by a scorpion the other night, my reaction wasn't exactly calm and orderly.

It was around nine thirty, and the dogs were barking at The Imaginary Thing That Isn't Behind The Diesel Shed, so Gaz was out front with the torch and I was walking across to the bathroom shed to get my shoes, when I felt a sharp nip on my big toe, like a bee sting. I knew straight away what it was, and sure enough, there was a good-sized scorpion, tail up, just next to my foot. "GARY! SCORPION BITE!" I yelled. I assumed that I was going to drop dead or start foaming at the mouth in paralysing convulsions at any second, but had the presence of mind to seize the nearest handy tourniquet - a dirty sock.

As I knotted it tight, Gaz ran in, grabbed the phone, yelled "DON'T PANIC!" and rang the hospital. "My lady's just been stung by a scorpion, should I bring her in?" "Yes." We grabbed the car and camp keys, shouting "DON'T PANIC!" at each other (as volunteer firefighters, we are trained to handle any kind of emergency). "Get the Fairlane keys! Don't panic!" said Gaz, stamping wildly at the scorpion. "There isn't enough petrol in it! I'm not panicking!" I yelled back, hopping frantically on one foot towards the car. "Okay, don't panic! I'll get the Landcruiser keys! Put the scorpion in a bag!" "The Landcruiser's full of stuff from the tip! Am I going to stop breathing? If I die, the internet banking codes are on the laptop!" "Don't panic! We'll take the ute! Jesus this thing's still moving!" "If I don't make it, remember to feed Smokey! He likes chicken! Where are the house keys?" "No need to panic! Get in the ute! Don't touch the scorpion!" "Oh my god it's still alive! It's trying to sting through the bag! If I go into a coma, there's a pen in my handbag you can use to give me an emergency tracheotomy!"

Still not panicking, Gaz drove at about two hundred kilometres an hour through the bush and we bounced out on to the highway. He even put the ute's yellow construction beacon on to warn other drivers that trained emergency responders were loose on the road. "The sock's not staying tight! What if the poison reaches my brain before we get into town?" "Don't panic! Hold on to the sock!" "Stop looking at it! You're going off the road!"

We got to the hospital without running anyone off the highway and were greeted by Cibu, who was on night shift. Coming from a foreign country where they have manners and are accustomed to thinking clearly due to a lifetime of not binge drinking, he was very calm. "No, I am very much not needing to be seeing the scorpion thank you very much," he said as we excitedly waved the bagged arachnid around the emergency room. "What is the reason for the tying of this sock around your foot please?"

The scorpion bite was quite exciting and all the night staff came in to have a look, hopefully asking if I felt my airways closing or was feeling any other interesting medical reactions to liven up a slow night. Disappointingly, I felt nothing other than a mild itching where the sting had got me, but Gary held my hand anyway and Sibu put an ice pack on my foot. After fifteen minutes of observations it was clear that the emergency resuscitation trolley wouldn't be needed, so Sibu had to settle for giving me some antihistamine and a tetanus shot in the ass, which cheered Gary up considerably. "Crikey! You should have seen how deep that went in!"

Anyway, I woke up alive in the morning and spent a fun-filled half hour googling scorpion facts. They aren't considered a serious bite in Australia, but it was an excellent bit of bush entertainment for the evening, and we learned the benefit of slovenly housekeeping habits, because you never know when a dirty old sock lying on the floor could save your life.

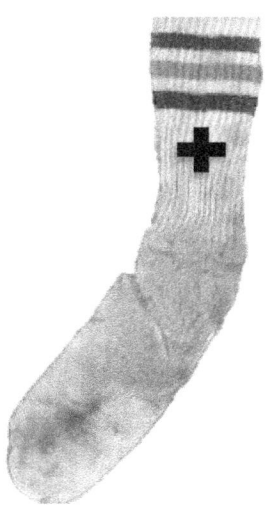

polite society

My family are coming to Meeka in April. Although it's only January, I and my handsome personal solar battery sequencer, Gary Hammer, have been excitedly preparing for the big hoe-down, disguising our spider-infested shed windows (or, as our friends call them, "holes") with anything we can find that resembles curtains, hiding the spare car parts under the bed and planning some surprise welcoming gestures, such as taking a shower the week before they get here.

Everything seemed under control until Mum started asking questions and we realised that despite dozens of emails, blogs, photos and phone calls, my family doesn't seem to have grasped some important aspects of Meekatharra, such as (a) where it is. Here is a rough transcript of my recent email correspondence with Mum:

reply <> mum@mumsemail.com.canada
Re: Visit
Hi Annakins, we have a few questions as we get ready to come and see you.

HI MUM, NO WORRIES MY REPLIES IN CAPS

1. Meeka sounds a bit rough and violent, is there somewhere nearby we can stay & just drive in?

WHAT MAP HAVE YOU BEEN LOOKING AT??

2. Do the shops have vegetarian food like tofurkey and Not Quite Chicken?

SHOPS?

3. Should we bring our bikes? How far is your place from the local coffee shop?

ABOUT SEVEN HUNDRED KILOMETRES

4. Should we bring our tennis racquets?

YES THEY WILL BE HANDY FOR SMASHING THE SCORPIONS IN THE BATHROOM

We realised that my family would quickly end up as a blood-streaked smear of tofu on the Great Northern Highway unless we could somehow prepare them - but I soon discovered it's impossible to convey what Meeka is like to city folks, because they think you're making it up. Giant insects the size of a small pet? Fifty degree heat? Large reptiles strolling by in the back yard?

Mum and my stepfather, Peter, are experienced, hardy travellers in their seventies who are extremely fit and enjoy various forms of exercise, even competing in triathlons and races, so they were hoping that Meeka would have some healthy outdoor activities until I explained that due to outback hazards such as heat, and beer, our local exercise options generally consist of Pub Fighting, Swearing At The Generator, Hiding From The Police, and Borrowing Craig's Ute So I Can Go To The Roadhouse For Some Smokes.

"It doesn't say anything about those on the website," said Mum on the phone. I looked around furtively. "We try to keep the good stuff a secret," I whispered.

My brother is a bit better prepared, having lived in Australia for many years now. "Remember, the more they abuse you, the more it means they like you" I reminded him. "Just say Mate and You B-----d a lot and you'll be right. And for god's sake don't wear a brand new Akubra or moleskins or anything like that, it doesn't look right on Canadians and you'll just get us, you know, shot or something."

With essential tourist survival information sorted out, my mind turned to the fact that this will be the first time Gary meets my family. "Do they realise we live in a shed and keep the spare teeth in a jar?" he asked. "I'm not sure," I replied. In Canada, a shed is kind of like what you see in movies, with clean happy cows and cheery faded red paint, while ours is more like Deliverance, but with extra scorpions and the newly-arrived Giant Racing Spiders, not to mention The Thing Living In Matt's Room Whose Eyes Glow In The Dark. To be on the safe side, I booked them into Paddy's Flat, which features many mod cons that we don't have at our place, such as electricity, and ceilings. Our friends were on emergency stand-by to look after them if we were at work, and Rocky generously offered to linger mysteriously in the bush around our camp dressed in red underpants and carrying a spear, standing on one leg with his foot balanced on his knee and gazing into the distance with a hidden boombox emitting didgeridoo sound effects to create a genuine outback tourism experience.

Realising that Gaz might be a bit nervous about meeting most of my family all in one go, I prepared a list of helpful tips, including Things Not To Mention Unless You Want To Cop An Earful, and I thought it might be helpful to share them with you in case you run into - or over - my family during their visit. Basically you want to try and avoid World News Of Any Kind, Gun Laws, Unusual Camping Gadgets, Pig Hunting, Religion, The War (they're originally from Britain, don't get them started) Manchester United, Manchester itself, Types Of Tofu, Sleeping Bag Temperature Tolerances and The Time My Brother Went Ice Climbing Oh God What Was He Thinking.

Then I realised - of course! that most of us won't be able to communicate clearly with my family anyway, due to our reliance on swear words for 98 percent of our verbal exchanges (the other 2 percent is non-verbal, or, as the police prefer to call it, "grievous bodily harm"). Canada has a reputation for being overly polite - it's the only country in the world where people use the word "beaver" in everyday conversation without sniggering - and I wondered what it would be like if we all tried to stop swearing while my family are visiting:

My Mum:
Hello! Can you tell me how to find the tennis court please?

Local Person 1:
Reproductive act!

My Mum:
I beg your pardon?

Local Person 2:
Apologies madam, my companion was merely indicating a state of alarum at being unexpectedly interrupted while engaging in the repair of this ill-bred canine's orifice of a generator motor.

My Mum:
Oh dear I'm sorry.

Local Person 2:
'Pon my word madam it is of no matter; I submit my humblest regrets at the fecal-headed verbal bumbling of this scurrilous scoundrel, to whom I shall now extend a fitting and just punishment for his grotesque social inadequacies by striking his wretched camel's digestive tract of a head with this splendidly weighty mechanical implement. The tennis courts are two streets up, on your left.

My Mum:
Thank you. What charming fellows!

But even though the eye-wateringly strong language you hear in Meeka could burn the ears off a monkey, it expresses the refreshingly direct, "get on with it" attitude of the resourceful, generous people who live here, the words of a place where there isn't time for city-life word-waffle; why shouldn't it be part of the tourist adventure?

Words are as much a part of our landscape as the mine pits, ghost towns and delightful hidden soaks & pools - the colourful nature of outback language is part of the people and the unpredictability that I think make Meekatharra such a delightfully rough diamond of a place, and it will mean a lot to share that with my family.

Of course we'll take them round to see the usual tourist sights, but to me it's the chaotic details of daily life out here that make it unique and memorable - so once my family arrive and we've taken them down to the courthouse to take out their first round of restraining orders, we want to share some of the wonderfully unexpected things you find yourself doing in Meeka, such as helping to fill ice cube bags at Norm's ice factory, giving old Nellie a lift home from Farmer Jack's, putting out a mattress fire at the creek, or joining an impromptu group discussion about which of the post office dogs ate Russell's sandwich.

Gary and I will do our best to ensure that they aren't left unsupervised, but if you see any of my family wandering off into the desert or Consul's Road with their tennis racquets and tofu sandwiches, just herd them gently into your back yard with a cup of tea and we'll come by to collect them. Don't worry about your p's and q's too much - in fact, I'm offering bonus beers to anyone who can work "dry as a dead dingo's donger" and "don't come the raw prawn" casually into a conversation during the big visit. Just try to keep a straight face, and if you see Rocky wandering through the bush from our place in a pair of red underpants, give him a lift home will ya?

Hammered

As many of you are aware, my handsome personal motor scooter mechanic Gary Hammer and I recently encouraged his son Matthew to escape from the hellish pits of Melton, Victoria and welcomed him to our charming desert bush hovel and the many attractions of Meekatharra.

"There's the historic Commercial Hotel," we pointed out as we drove through town. "And the court house is just over there when it's time for you to take out your first round of restraining orders."

After a quick tour it was time for Matt to get to work. No lazing around by the pool! "But I've been up and travelling since four a.m.," protested Matt. "You'll be right," we said encouragingly. "Here, see if this firefighting uniform fits, then go round and fix the 27 sink taps at Paddy's. Don't forget to pick up a drum of diesel on your way back. If Margie isn't at the fuel yard just drive around until you see her or Ronnie, he's usually driving the forklift, or go and ask at the pub and while you're there give Meacho some money for that carton we got last week, then pop up to the roadhouse and ask Judy what time you're starting tomorrow morning. Remember you need to juggle your roadhouse hours around cleaning for Jo. Here's $2.50 for your lunch. Don't talk to any women at the bar."

With Matt's employment situation sorted out, Gary and I went home for a well-earned weekend nap. We were both pleased and excited to have

Matt staying with us, and it was nice to see how much support I received from the Meeka community as I began my journey as a first time parental role model (having forgotten to have children of my own earlier in life thank god). "You poor thing," people said. "Now you have to put up with two of them."

But I was optimistic about Matt's arrival. Two Hammers! They would be able to talk to each other about cars and motorcycles and all the other things that poor Gary is forced to talk with me about in lieu of someone who understands him.

"Look at this!" Gary will exclaim as he bursts in to the kitchen. "The original solenoid pro-turbo spondometer was missing a globulator, they cost a fortune but I made one myself by cutting this old carburettor modulatoriser down to 3 mil then vulcanising it to fit the point oh-seven series injector, now all I have to do is take the fathomiser out of that Yamaha we found at the tip and I'll be able to run it from the fuel pump to the 12 volt transferometer!"

Then he proudly holds out a small black oily thing which is suspiciously similar to something I vacuumed up from the lounge room floor a week earlier and I try to be cheerfully supportive while ignoring the nagging guilty feeling that I may have caused the problem in first place when I was cleaning up and - silly woman! - mistook a pile of filthy old motorcycle parts lying under to the sofa for (gasp) junk.

But my dreams of a tech-talk-free existence dissipated in a haze of diesel fumes as I discovered that I now had a two-headed Hammer monster on my hands - it came home from the tip, grimy and excited, both of its heads talking at the same time:

Gary:
Look! I found this old Honda thermonuclear coupling device for the pandalometer!

Matt:
Here's a solar twin-V disconjoineriser I can use to fix the helicopter engine!

Me:
We have a helicopter engine?

Gary:
We found three! And part of a point 2-mil Holden valve grinding polariser!

Matt:
This looks like part of an incredulometer. My feet are hot. Do I have any Telstra credit left?

Gary:
I think this is a grommet adjuseriser, but it's broken. Have you seen my pants? I'm hungry.

Making a mental note to see if I could get hold of a taser on eBay, I congratulated my happy hunters on their wonderfully useful tip finds, then went back to my household chores of smacking the scorpions in the lounge room with a shovel and googling Common Deadly Poisonous Snakes Of WA Especially That Large Brownish-Green Snake That You Nearly Stepped On This Morning By The Hills Hoist. I didn't tell Matt about the snake, because Matt was still trying to cope with his nightly adventures in our lizard-infested guest shed.

"There's a bungarra in my room," whispered Matt, waking us up in the wee hours with haunted eyes. "It'll just be a gecko," I said. "They're small and harmless." Matt shook his head. "No, it's definitely a bungarra, one of those big ones, like they have in Indonesia." "What, a Komodo dragon?" I asked. "Yeah, like that. Big. I can hear its claws on the roof." Matt shivered, and Gary moaned in his sleep. "It's just a gecko, go to bed," I ordered and rolled over.

We were woken again about half an hour later. "What are you doing??" I grumbled. "Setting a trap," said Matt. I gave up and went back to keeping Gary awake with my snoring, but in the morning when I went to collect Matt's laundry I saw that he'd surrounded his bed with mouse traps and placed hefty cans of Mortein within reach. I had visions of waking up one night to the sounds of an enraged bungarra flailing about the room with mouse traps flapping on its feet, maddened by the Mortein in its eyes, and Matt clinging terrified to top of the wardrobe. I made a mental note to see if I could get hold of a tranquiliser gun on eBay.

Lizards aside, Matt took to Meeka like the proverbial and in his first couple of weeks he managed to get a job at the roadhouse, buy a car off Rocky, take over several of Jo's cleaning jobs, make a good impression on the Meeka ladies, build several display stands for my souvenir business, get on to a first name basis with the truckies and locals at the roadhouse, join the fire brigade, repair one of Gaz's old motorbikes and unblock our kitchen sink while texting everyone in the known universe every hour on the hour and then slipping into a well-earned coma for his weekly ration of twenty minutes' sleep, his thumb still going at 72 words per minute on his overheating phone.

"He'll be the next Norm Trenfield at this rate!" I marvelled to Gaz as we spent a quiet, romantic evening searching for the banded desert snake that had taken up residence in the tool room, and whose babies had hatched and were sporadically appearing from under the TV bench during episodes of "River Monsters". Gary was proud of the way his young bloke was taking to Meeka, and the nightly screams from Matt's room gradually died down. "I think I'm getting used to the lizards!" reported Matt cheerfully. I had visions of him sitting up in bed with the bungarra, teaching it how to send text messages.

The next day Matt and I went into town to get his police check and grab a few groceries. Matt thought that this would involve driving into town, doing what we planned to do, then driving home again. But as all you locals know, there is no such thing as "just popping down to the shop" in Meeka, and Matt got a wonderful introduction to the rich, unpredictable joys of outback time mismanagement.

On the way, we took some rubbish to the tip, and discovered a bunch of really good stuff we would probably never use, so we took the new rubbish home, then set off again, this time actually reaching the post office, where we found that the stubby holders I'd designed for Darcy had arrived, so we took them over to the corner store, then watched some Thai music videos in Darcy's office until I remembered that I needed to go to the chemist to collect George's souvenir order, so we wandered over there and spent about twenty minutes chatting with everyone in the queue about the rain and the wretched midgie bites everyone's been suffering from aren't they a bugger have you tried putting vinegar on them?

Then we went to Farmer Jack's and in between chatting with various neighbours and mates in the aisles managed to get about 7% of the shopping done, at which point we remembered that we forgot to get the police check form, but on the way back to the post office we stopped at Coates Hire to see if Gaz wanted a pie and Tony said he had World War Z on DVD and we could get it from Anne at their place, but on the way to Anne & Tony's we see old Paddy walking along in the broiling sun so we give him a lift to Byron's place...What's that Paddy? You're not staying there anymore? Where are you staying now? You're not sure? We'll drive around until we see it OK?...then we dropped him off at Leanne's mum's place where I confused him even more by asking if they still had the guinea pigs, then we zipped round to get the DVD off Anne but she'd gone back inside so we went back to Coates and Tony rang her up and we went back again and she handed the DVD through the back gate a bit covered in slobber from the excited guard dog, then we went to the roadhouse to get a pie for Gaz and half an hour later we're still hanging around yarning with the truckies and Gaz's pie has gone cold OMG that reminds me we forgot about the ice cream in the back seat so we rush back to our camp, fire up the genny, turn the freezer on, unload the groceries and sit down for a lovely cold drink then remember that we never got the police check form which is what we went to town for in the first place but we don't care because on the way we got a zombie DVD, advice on how to improve a lemon tree, a remedy for midgie bites, a list of available puppies, some old weed-whacker parts and a rumour that there might be a spare rear spoiler for Matt's car at Dave's place.

"That's Meeka," I explained. "It's grouse!" said Matt, which I understand is a phrase that young people use to express approval, or maybe it's a phone app. Anyway, it was great to see how young Matt embraced the challenges that Meeka threw at him, and the way his hard-working, generous nature was welcomed into the daily flow of life in our little town - a big change from the frustrations of city life.

Matt's back in Melbourne at the moment having his broken foot tended to (that's a whole other story), but we look forward to having him back in a few weeks' time and introducing him to the giant racing spiders and other critters that have appeared in the house since the cyclone rain. You'll need to excuse me now - the bungarra's texting us from Matt's room. I think it wants help with its Facebook page.

The Finance Retort

I was watching the news the other night with my handsome personal karate expert, Gary Hammer, and once again there were people in suits talking about The Budget, which is apparently three gazillion dollars in deficit with a something or other index of 1.9 on the Footy or the Nastysick, which I think means that we accidentally gave a whole heap of money to Spain or Collingwood or maybe someone left the government wallet on the counter at the pub. Anyway, we owe a whole heap of money and unless everyone starts chain-smoking like mad and - literally - coughing up the tax dough, no one's sure where we're going to get more.

But I want to know how we got into so much debt in the first place. Who do we owe the money to? How come they keep lending it to us? When do they want it back? And do they have large threatening bikie-gang mates who'll kick the door down at three in the morning to take all the furniture if we don't keep up our payments?

Many of us do go into debt, because we want the nice new shiny things we see on the TV which we can get on interest-free credit from Harvey Norman, but it's pretty hard for the average person to rack up much more than a typical mortgage and a few thousand bucks on the credit card before the bank says "No" and you say "Bugger" and go home and see if there's anything round the back of the shed you can flog to Wazza next pension day.

The government's already tried this, flogging off our utilities with the inevitable result that we all now pay 163 percent of our income on electricity bills (that's if we only use the toaster once a week) and some of the most expensive phone rates in the universe. But despite more and more money being dragged from our screaming wallets, our hospitals are still trying to keep their old cat scan machines going with duct tape and a hammer, while the government keeps spending millions of dollars on new carpets for Parliament House or a fighter jet or something.

Now, if the government was your husband, you'd be really cross:

Missus:
I sent you to the shop for milk and bread, and you've blown it all on this fighter jet!

Hubby:
The repayments are only fifty thousand a week, anyway it's awesome, it's got a 17.2 litre turbo charged injector system, titanium alloy tappet bearings and--

Missus:
Take. It. Back.

Hubby:
But--

Missus:
And take the rubbish on your way out.

How come our own governments can't use the same common sense that most of us seem to manage each day? Are they sending the wrong person to the shop? Because really, it's pretty simple - if you have X amount of money, you can buy X amount of stuff, right? And you put the bread & milk in the shopping trolley first, then maybe grab a packet of Tim

Tams for a treat and hope that there's enough left to buy a pack of smokes and if there isn't you put the Tim Tams back and go and humbug some ciggies off Wazza because he still owes you for that genny casing you sold him from out of the shed when he said had that extra cash for fixing that washing machine that Craig's missus got off Baz's missus.

But it's all made elaborately mysterious with the bewildering jibber jabber of the economic experts, and in our confusion we somehow go along with it, glazed over with boredom and incomprehension as global national debt figures reach ludicrous numbers like 16 trillion dollars (that's the current US debt). It's all just numbers on the computers, held up by our belief that the little squiggles on the screen represent these enormous amounts of money, which is silly, because 16 trillion dollars doesn't actually exist - you couldn't physically fit 16 trillion dollars on the entire planet, let alone in your handbag.

It's all made up by corporate sociopaths who have nothing better to do than create insanely complex, loop-holed money games. Can't they just go to the pub like everyone else? I reckon we should all just pitch in and build them some sheds. As all women know, a shed will keep a bloke occupied and out of your hair for days at a time, with a 50/50 chance of him emerging around tea time with something useful such as a solar battery charger or a 12 volt lighting system so complicated that you have to sit in the dark until he gets home to activate the invertalometer so there's enough kilobytes to run the frequency modulatoriser but turn the red switch on before you rotate the black dial to the left or it will set fire to the washing machine.

Anyway, I think we'd all agree that the government could use some everyday common sense, and where better to find this than in Meeka? But writing to them won't help; they need indexes, figures and jibber jabber, so maybe I'll start sending them my Weekly Meeka Finance Report:

"Gidday, Shazza here with the latest Meekanomic figures. Bashed-up old tin from the tip has risen to five chooks a sheet due to an unexpected drop in vacant houses being trashed by drunken parties. Old starter motors have dropped by 0.3 favours to a mate, while those tyres round the back of

Grunter's place have risen by six stubbies of Carlton Cold. The latest poll shows local business confidence going up, down, up, down, then around the corner to drop a genny off for Norm and finally wandering off to the Commie for a counter meal. The MSFI (Meeka Street Fight Index) is currently at 7.2 punches per carton, which has pushed the FDSR (Flying Doctor Stress Rating) to a yearly high of 4.2 glasses of sav-blanc and a long snooze on the sofa, resulting in a welcome 27.3 per cent increase in Panadol sales from Farmer Jack's. Dog prices remain steady at one carton per red heeler if you can catch Roy at home. We'll switch live now to Bush Camp finance reporter Anna for the domestic figures - Anna, I understand there's good news in this week's camp index percentages?"

"That's right Shazza. A 32 percent increase in the Gary Hammer Repair Index has boosted 1 refueling of the generator by an additional cup of tea and a sandwich, the bush camp chihuahua is in bullish territory with 3.7 imaginary burglar attacks, while Red Dog's credit rating has plummeted to minus 5 as a result of eating Gary's sock, twice, but this has been positively off-set by a rise of 2.3 points on the Barking At The Cockatoos Eating The TV Aerial chart. Gross scorpion totals are holding steady at 1.2 seasonal bathroom incidents and the global value of A Spectacular Full Moon Rising Over The Desert remains priceless."

But really, as I drive through the bush and into town each day, I don't need a finance report or polls to tell me the value of things - I can see them for myself. Look - there's where we put out the scrub fire next to the bakery; there's Adam, putting a new gate up at the Royal; Margie, watering the lawns at the racecourse, Rigby tending the street plants, Constable Mark helping some kids with the bike pump, Andrew filling the freezer at Norm's ice factory, Meacho and the Coffee Club waving from their chairs in front of the Commie, Elaine taking someone to the hospital in the ambulance, Svjena taking wildflower photos for the CRC postcards, Steve and Jock coming in dusty and tired from grading the Wiluna road, Helen helping Robyn into the hostel van, Russell and Bindie lugging the daily mail into the post office, Jo vacuuming the court house, Ronnie cruising through town with another forklift delivery, Tristan and his work crew up on the Yulella Vision roof - everyone going about their busy day, keeping the town going, but not too busy to wave gidday, stop for a chat, pat the dog or lend a hand when it's needed.

So I'm not going to bother anymore with what they say on the news with all their debt indexes and consumer confidence ratings, because we're surrounded by a spectacularly beautiful landscape, people who care about the town, heaps of stuff behind the shed and mates to help you out - and you can't put a price on that.

# of meat and men

It's been a few years now, so I think it's safe to talk about it. I've used disguised names just in case, because we all became involved one way or another, and I bet there's still a frozen prawn or two in someone's freezer that could lead to some awkward questions. You could be eating one right now. Does it taste good? You bet. Because there's nothing like a free lunch, and this was the mother of all free lunches.

You know what I'm talking about. I was there. You were there. Even people who weren't there were there, or were nearly there, or heard about it from someone who knew someone who was mates with someone who was there. For three days it was a madness that gripped the town as greed and the heady aroma of spilled beer threatened to unravel decades-old mateships. Families turned against each other. Men wept. Dogs celebrated. For a little while, it was bigger than the gold rush.

It was The Great Truck Rollover.

I had only been in Meeka for a couple of weeks, living in B---'s spare donger with T--- as I waited for my Main Street house purchase to go through. This was in the days - how impossibly long ago it seems! - before I met my handsome personal shed builder, Gary Hammer. Little did I know it, but I was about to be introduced to full-blast Meeka Madness, and it was an experience that cemented my realisation that I was in a far more interesting place than anything listed on the WA Tourism website. I've transcribed these notes from the diary I was keeping at the time:

DAY 1:

A food delivery road train has rolled a trailer on the other side of town. Neighbours rush to the scene with utes and trucks to help with the clean-up in true outback "lend a hand" style.

"No worries mate! We'll load up the local trucks and take it to the tip for ya!" Camaraderie and mateship warm the hearts of all.

DAY 2:

It's evident from the suspicious appearance of stray potatoes and oranges on Meeka side streets that helpful locals have employed a rather loose interpretation of the phrase "take it all to the tip". And why not? Outback folk are genetically incapable of throwing anything out - after all, the tip is where you go to get things, not chuck stuff out! Truckloads of vegies and food have been happily distributed to animals and old people. Sacks of fruit are cheerfully handed over neighbours' fences. Women roll up their sleeves and begin chopping, boiling and freezing the hip-high piles of produce. It's like harvest season, and everyone gladly lends a hand.

But as the men begin to unload their trucks, rumblings of concern emerge. "Oi. Anyone seen that pallet of bacon?" "Pallet? I found a 2 kilo box." "What about them prawns mate?" "They went to the tip mate." "Nah, didn't Kev have em on the back of his ute mate?" "Dunno mate. I can't find me box of sausages either mate." Men begin to look sideways at each other in the pub.

T--- comes home looking grim. "Something's up," he says darkly. "I 'ad three tubs of them Italian cheeses put aside an no one's seen em."

I stir my giant pots of Random Roadside Vegetable Soup and try to look sympathetic through the steam. We are each having 27 lamb chops for dinner, because there is no more room in the fridge. Backyard barbecues smoke out the town as night falls and men gather to exchange notes on who got what. Stories emerge of "hundreds" of cases of beer which have mysteriously gone missing, and no one knows what happened to the alleged crates of sirloin strips which no one actually remembers seeing in the first place. Women continue making vats of soup and using mallets to wedge food into overloaded fridges. Stars fill the night sky as the men of the town snore into an uneasy sleep, dreaming of missing steaks while dozens of dogs fart contentedly amid piles of barbecue bones.

DAY 3

Men continue to go to the tip in search of the mythical mountain of prawn cases. "It was only 18 degrees last night mate, the ones at the bottom should be OK." Conspiracy theories spread wildly as blokes drive slowly around, spying over each other's fences, peering not-so-discreetly into each other's ute trays, and dropping round to compare stories.

"I reckon someone did a deal with the truck driver over them cases of beer mate." "Yer, and I reckon it's real suss that Wazza's got that old cool room of his running, why would he need all that space if he only took one box a them sausages like 'e said mate?"

T--- spends the morning looking for the missing cheeses, but comes home with a case of prawns ("don't tell anyone!") and a promise from G--- that we can have some of "them porterhouses" from his freezer in exchange for not telling B--- about a block of land that B--- thinks G--- is going to sell him but G--- has already agreed to sell it to R---, or something (I stop listening as I google-search for recipes that require 173 eggs). Like the pots of soup on every stove, the blokes of the town slowly seethe towards boiling point with simmering rumours and bursting bubbles of hot air.

I take a ten litre bucket of soup over to H--- & P---'s house in exchange for some spare rib bones for the dogs, who have already eaten nearly five times their own body weight in burnt chop fat; the combined farting from blokes and dogs at our donger defies any efforts with the air freshener spray and the place smells like a charnel pit. H---'s husband S--- comes round, muttering about "them crates of sirloin strips" which "someone must have taken off G---'s truck because G--- says 'e hasn't seem em and B--- reckons 'e loaded em on with them barramundi fillets but I only found one box so I reckon that bastard's got em somewhere'. T--- sits staring into the barbecue fire, a cheeseless, broken man.

Every portable fridge, esky, caravan freezer and cool room in town has been plugged in to overheating powerboards; sacks of potatoes and carrots sit under sprinklers in people's yards to keep cool while us women-folk keep making astonishing quantities of soup which we take round to each other's houses only to be handed a vat of more homemade soup in exchange.

At last the crash site and the tip are picked clean and weary women gratefully put their chopping boards away. Children gaze despondently at dinner plates piled high with broccoli. Overstuffed freezers are held shut with straining ratchet straps, the smoke of a hundred barbecues dissipates into the heat-weary haze of the outback sunset and dogs lie groaning and barely conscious in every yard.

But amid the glorious cornucopia there's a rotten egg and a fishy smell - what happened to the cheeses? Where did the barramundi go? Was there really a whole pallet of sirloin strips, and who took them? Did F--- secretly trade them to W--- to give to J--- to hide in his mobile cool room and did B---'s missus put them up to it?

The deepest bonds of the outback grow frayed as rumour begets rumour and neighbours prowl each other's fencelines. It's comedy and tragedy. It's Banjo Patterson, it's Henry Lawson. Ted Egan could make a ballad out of it. Slim Dusty would have had a field day. It's the Town With No Prawns. It's The Grog And The Barra Box, Clancy Of The Where'd It Go. It's man versus himself, pitted against his own venal nature and discovering that his moral code of mateship, loyalty and the shaking of hands is worth less than a cryovacced pack of scotch fillets and a carton of beer.

As the sun sinks into the western sky, the last sad prawn hunters straggle back from the tip empty-handed, the soup vats are washed clean and men frown grimly into their Sunday night beers, contemplating meat, mates and payback.

Meeka Montage

The familiar roar of the road trains passing, carrying gigantic mining parts - a single wheel as big as a house, engines as big as a bus. Kids yelling and laughing up and down the street. Gings. Bare feet on the fifty-degree tarmac. The clunk of the ice-making machine. Distant booms of thunder and flashes of dry lightning. A lazily-raised "gidday" wave and a toot toot from the car horn as someone you know drives past. The sound of dogs and people fighting (together?) from the government house across the laneway. Stop for a chat and a glass of water over the fence. Squirt the kids with the hose. Smile and remember the days before you got too old to run around like a joyful wild thing in your underpants. Water fights. The crunch of an ice cube in your mouth. Grown-ups busy, hot and cross.

A dust cloud rises on the far Wiluna road. Wind your windows up. It's Millsy in the water tanker. Wave. Wind the window down again. A joke on the two-way. Static from the trucks on the Great Northern. "Southbound...southbound..." Red Dog leaning so far out the window that his paws are on the side mirror, tongue flapping dry in the scorching midday sun. If he could drive, he would. We go and sit in Garden Gully creek like crocodiles, bubbling under old straw hats.

Flies sucking at your eyes. Tiny frogs hop past the bed on their way to the pool. Sweat drops from your face on to the floor as you work. Squirting saline solution and pawpaw ointment up your nose because it's so dry your nasal passages crack and bleed. It'll be months before you know what a cold shower feels like. Craving. Anything cold, wet, beery, icy . . . "Fifty-six on the forecourt!" says Richard as he comes dusty and sweat stained into the roadhouse. Walking into the blast furnace of Outside to get lovely lovely bags of ice from the coldbox. Watch your icy pole steam away to nothing thirty seconds after you take it from the freezer.

Red arms and neck and pale white chest. Your bloke. How he does it, twelve hour days in this heat, as tough and beat-up as the machines he drives. Skin desperately sucking up the moisture as you sink ahhhhh into the pool after work. Hand us a beer love. Think it'll rain? Nah. Fans creakily wafting air over Smokey who's lying flat on his back like he's been shot. Spiny double gees and bindies stab your bare feet, as tough & sharp as steel needles. The garden looks like how you feel. Red dust in everything. Geckos and ta-ta lizards dart in and out of the house; honeyeaters, finches and wagtails lurk near the pond, working up the courage to swoop a drink. Dogs follow the shade around the houses, too hot to bark at strangers. Ants in the food bowls. Strange insects at night. The smell of meat on a barbie.

Heading off to Five Mile mine pit with your mates for a swim. Take the new barmaid from the Commie. Never seen anything like it, doesn't trust half the stories you tell her. They won't believe this back in Ireland/Germany/Pommieland. Facebook images of a life that seems like a dream, or hell, or something in between. "Yer get used to it." Saving up so they can get away. Then coming back, because there's something about Meeka . . .

Just before sunset you can feel the heat of the day baking up off the ground and it feels as if it will never be cool again. The wind drops. Gunmetal blue storm clouds rise on the horizon. A red sky. A stumbling stream of people drifting home as the pubs close. The warm silence of night, restful after a day of hot wind and dust. People and dogs heat-worn and asleep under air conditioners, on camp beds, in gardens, pub balconies, truck cabs or on a blanket by the creek. A family of emus slowly crosses Main Street and disappears into the scrub. Stillness. Stars.

the CAMPING TRIP part one

My handsome personal auto electrician Gary Hammer and I decided to have a holiday. "Let's go bush!" we said. "But you already live in the bush," our friends pointed out. "We're going to different bush," we explained as we crammed 1.2 tonnes of mostly unnecessary camping gear into our old Toyota. "Bush that doesn't have the annoyances of modern life, such as air conditioning, level sleeping surfaces or nearby emergency rescue services."

We set off up the Mt. Clere road towards Mount Augustus, stopping only twice so that Gary could use his excellent supply of tools and strong language to repair the car. En route we encountered scenic creek crossings, a startled bustard, Jareth, 60 billion flies and menopause. It escapes me now why we decided to go camping in hot summer weather with no air conditioning, hormone replacement therapy patches or antipsychotic drugs, but fortunately Gary is an experienced bush traveller, and as the car interior temperature climbed past 48 degrees and I began having homicidal hot flushes (or 'power surges' as we call them) every five minutes, he made sure he had a ready supply of hunting knives and heavy blunt instruments at hand in case I needed help "cooling down" as they recommend in the menopause support pamphlets.

In the traditional way of car camping with no itinerary in mind, we drove for hours and hours and hours and hours while I said "Let's stop here" and "This looks good for camping" every fifteen minutes and Gary ignored me, his fists clenched around the steering wheel, eyes glazed over in a thousand-yard stare. You ladies know what I mean. Once at the wheel, a bloke will keep driving even if he's unconscious or actually dead. This is because when a man gets into a car, it triggers the ancient Woolly Mammoth Hunter part of his brain, which tells him he must outrun the other predators, kill the prey and then drag it back to the cave where, hopefully, a woman will be waiting with a cook pot.

The problem in modern life of course is that all the elements are mixed up. The bloke already has the woman in the car, which is also a bit like a cave, but there's no woolly mammoth, so his lower brain tells him he needs to get in the confusing car/cave and look for one to kill, but of course there are no woolly mammoths anymore and he drives and drives, his subconscious cruelly taunting him to *Find The Prey!*, speeding past the other cars on the road so that they can't get to the woolly mammoth before he does, and now the woman is getting annoyed and it's all wrong, wrong, wrong, but he's locked helplessly in Primal Hunt mode. The only way to make him stop is with the camp frying pan, or That Tone Of Voice, the one that all blokes instinctively recognise: "Stop. The Car. Now."

At last we just swerved off the track into the bush and threw our brand new dome swag out on the nearest bit of flat ground, then lay in pools of our own sweat as the breathless night heat slowly gave way to a fan-forced oven of dawn sun and millions of flies, many of which we had for breakfast. After a quick look at Mt. Augustus ("that's a big rock") and Cattle Pool ("is that a dead cow?"), we headed northeast on the scenic, little-used Pingandy track.

Our friend Paul, who is a keen outdoorsman, once asked us what would be the most useful tool he could take for remote bush camping. "Gary," I promptly replied. "He's a human Swiss Army knife." And it was a good thing that Gaz did come along on our holiday, because it was on the most isolated and flood-prone section of the Pingandy track, with a big fat storm cell approaching, that our elderly Landcruiser decided to catch fire.

Now, contrary to what most women think, it does not help a bloke when you say things like "What's wrong with it", "How long will it take to fix" or "I told you we should have taken the other road, now we're going to die" when he is trying to deal with a holiday car problem. I have complete faith in Gary and I knew he would figure out a solution, so I just let him do his thing and wandered off to look at the scenery, which consisted mainly of trackless hot rocky wastes and an occasional small dead bush. Gary had gone uncharacteristically quiet, and enormous black sheets of rain were visible on the horizon. It was obvious that we were going to die. At least we had lots of water and food, so we'd be comfortable until the raging flash floods swept us away like helpless prawns.

Just as I was completely absorbed by catastrophic imaginings of clinging to the Landcruiser as raging torrents battered us with dead cows and entire trees, our fingertips slowly slipping from each other as we shrieked "I love you!" while the muddy waters dragged us under, I heard the car start. My hero! He won't admit it, but Gaz is a genius.

With the car not in flames and neither of us dead from heat stroke or floods, we happily headed off on to the Ashburton Downs Road, which is really a goat track chopped up by about 60 million washouts, and very slow going. About 734 hours later, moaning and delirious from night driving ("Where the ---- are we?? How long is this stupid track? Did we die and this is hell? Look, a dingo") we pulled out on the tarmac west of Paraburdoo, hoping to find a motel and air conditioning, but Paraburdoo was closed so we camped out of town, had a refreshing bucket wash and woke up next to a cow.

NEXT MONTH: We look at ancient Burrup Peninsula petroglyphs, crazy hilarious Dampier locals convince us to try and deliberately destroy our car, we find The Cougar, and a kangaroo washes our dishes.

Our Bush Camp

The Pingandy Track - a scenic place to die

Python Pool, bristling with piranhas

Young male camels looking for lost tourists to eat

the CAMPING TRIP part TWO

Clink. Clink. rustlerustlerustle. Clink. CRASH. Clink rustlerustlerustle shlurpshlurpshlurp.

A pair of furry clown feet and a long fat tail were just visible behind the Landcruiser. Clink clink CRASH shlurpshlurp. My half-awake brain finally registered: a rather large kangaroo, half inside our car. But why was it doing the dishes? Another plate fell to the ground and I could hear cutlery being shifted around - torchlight revealed the roo trying to drink from our washing-up bucket, where I'd left the dinner dishes to soak overnight. "Here, stop making such a racket," I said, handing it a bowl of water. "Whaazza?" asked Gary. "Just a kangaroo doing the dishes," I replied. "Ahhargh," moaned Gaz and we settled down again, the gentle shoreline sounds of Ningaloo Reef sending us off to sleep.

We'd finally abandoned the baking hot north Pilbara for Exmouth and Cape Range National Park, camping at the mouth of Yardie Creek and spending our mornings snorkeling in Turquoise Bay. Beach kangaroos were plentiful, and we were serenaded each morning by the delicate, complex songs of a family of butcher birds, who were quite impressed with our efforts to join in. Late afternoons featured the entertainment of foolhardy four wheel drivers becoming bogged in the deep sand of the creek mouth crossing, something we'd decided not to do, having already made an idiotic 4x4 spectacle of ourselves on the Burrup Peninsula.

Our trip so far featured the horrors of Karratha, the vast and spectacular Hamersley Ranges, and Python Pool in Millstream Chichester National Park. Because it's a world-famous attraction, Python Pool has virtually no signage indicating how to find it, and when we arrived there with visions of outback frolicking and camping, the adjacent camping area had burnt down. Python Pool was absolutely beautiful and a welcome relief from the searing daytime heat, but if they ever do decide to put some signs up they might want to include one that says "DANGER!! FEROCIOUS CARNIVOROUS PIRANHA-LIKE FISH WHICH WILL SET UPON YOU IN A BLOOD-CRAZED FEEDING FRENZY!! Please take your litter with you thank you." My handsome personal navy munitions retrieval diver, Gary Hammer, was gnawed in several tender areas by these deceptively small, blood-crazed piscatorial pests. It was like one of those episodes of Star Trek where they land on a pretty, Eden-like garden planet but the flowers suddenly grow teeth and the guy with no last name gets eaten before the first ad break.

Anyway, with night falling and a huge bush fire-front raging southwest of Port Hedland, we abandoned our camping plans and decided to find a cheap motel in Roebourne. Ha ha! When we got there, we saw no evidence of any living beings and a peculiar darkness enveloped most of the town. It was like a scene from The Walking Dead. We did see one bloke, but he was running, possibly for his life. "Let's try Karratha," said Gaz as we nervously checked our door locks.

We grimly headed on to Karratha, which features many deceptive signs such as "MOTEL" and "CARAVAN PARK" that lead you into derelict industrial areas and prison-like mine accommodation camps. I finally resorted to googling and found a motel which happily organised a five-year mortgage plan to cover the cost of an overnight stay. The good old days of just coming across a cheap 'n' cheerful motel room are gone in WA - it's all about the mighty mining dollar.

The next morning we braved the traffic lights and busy busy people to stuff ourselves sick at McDonalds ("God this stuff is disgusting...are you going to finish those chips?"), and headed off to Dampier, where we discovered former Meeka resident Tina Storer, who runs the Seaman's Mission, a charming little shop and hangout for wandering sailors, and a great place to get a cold drink and directions into the Burrup Peninsula, where, as Tina assured us, it would be fun to destroy our car.

The Burrup Peninsula, or "Murujuga", is most widely known because of the LNG plant, but it should be a household name because of the ancient petroglyphs (rock engravings). It is the largest and oldest rock art site in the world - there are images of mega fauna that died out over 45,000 years ago - and it is also the site of a terrible massacre of aboriginal people, known as the "Flying Foam Massacre". Over 60 Yapururra people were shot by white "settlers" when they tried to exact justice over the rape of a Yapururra woman assaulted by a white police officer - but there are no tourist signs or information about any of that.

Even a shire ranger who stopped to see if we were lost knew virtually nothing about the age, importance or history of the area. There are plenty of signs leading you to the LNG visitor centre - a huge, ugly factory complex hacked jarringly into the unique and spectacular rocky landscape - but not a single sign or scrap of information about the ancient human heritage to be seen. If you want to know about the real history of this area, get hold of a video called "Exile and The Kingdom" which was made by Roeburne locals - I found it a compelling, engrossing documentary about the heritage and experiences of the aboriginal people in the area, made in a calmly observational manner that makes the actions of the colonial invaders (past and present) all the more horrific.

The petroglyphs are incredible, and extensive. You could spend days rambling the rocky terrain, discovering images of animals, sea creatures and mysterious symbols. A major campaign had to be fought to preserve any of the rock art, and over 25% of it has been lost to industrial development. To me, it's just another reminder that if you got an average group of normal everyday citizens together, people like you and me, we'd say there was no question, the place needs to be preserved - and celebrated! But when it's politicians and big business, it's a different story...it honestly defies belief, to see that big ugly gas plant with its proud "Visitor Centre" sign, probably cemented right into the very ground where ancient, intricate artwork once stood. Welcome to civilisation.

After rambling among the artwork, the heat took its toll and we moved on to the next attraction: the "Jump Up", a dramatic 4x4 climb leading to an alluring secluded beach. Now, if we'd followed Tina's directions properly we would have indeed got over the Jump Up, but we kind of went off on the wrong track, and got ourselves stuck on something which we later discovered was called The Tin Opener or The Eviscerator or something.

We did get out and look before we attempted the 87 degree rock-jagged slope. "I don't like it," I said. "Me neither," said Gaz. "I don't think we should do it," I said. "No," agreed Gaz. We got in the car, where we had one of our odd silent mind-reading moments, and without a further word, Gaz gunned our faithful old Toyota straight up the ragged incline. Yahoo!

We nearly made it. But our cheering was suddenly interrupted by a nasty noise. You know, that kind of tearing/crunching/snapping sort of sound that is not good to hear coming from a car. We'd snapped some doovers in the whatsit, not the axle but the other thingamabobs, so one wheel wasn't working. "Bugger." We glanced around to see if anyone was watching. "We meant to do that!" Gary wrestled our poor Landcruiser out of the hill track and we limped back to the public beach, where Gaz deftly rearranged various parts to do a temporary fix on the busted wheel while I helped by reading and falling asleep. Some locals parked nearby, got out a carton of red cans, and watched. A few fishing folk drove slowly past. No one said anything, but still we burned with shame - two more tourist idiots who tried to do the Jump Up!

On our way back into Karratha for replacement parts, we discovered, on a busy corner, The Cougar. Meeka locals will recall the bubbly and indefatigable Narelle, who set up her Cougar Kitchen food van in Meeka last year. Still going strong and doing a roaring trade, she now has a "drive thru", and I stayed for a good long chin wag & prawn twisters while Gaz, always my car repair hero, went to the Toyota shop.

There were many other great moments as we made our way along the coast - giving a tin of Mortein to a bloke and his young son who were travelling in a tiny Brumby ute infested with fire ants, banging away on the strange iron rocks on the Landor road which sound just like bells when you hit them with a hammer, floating along in schools of jewel-coloured fish in Ningaloo Reef, exploring the lost mysteries of old homestead ruins. The traces of the past always make me wonder if, with our modern 4x4's and google maps, we see more and experience less?

The funny thing was that nearly everywhere we stopped, we met someone who once lived in Meeka. "Is old so and so still there?" they'd ask. "Who's cooking at the pub now?" It was oddly reassuring, as if Meeka was our home planet in the centre of our ramblings, a beacon in the vast landscape. It was good to finally come home to our shed, our friends and our camp dogs, who intensely sniffed us all over as if to say, "Well, where have you been?"

# of golf balls and balloons

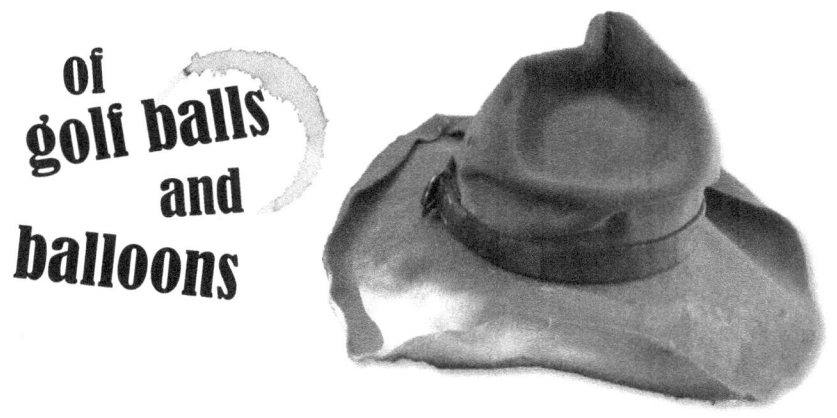

This is for Kerry, who keeps on going

Our little town has had a heartbreaking June and July - one funeral after another, saying goodbye to folks who were loved, respected and treasured, not just by their families and friends, but by our whole community. We've also had some bad press in the media due to a recent and tragic criminal act of domestic violence, which can never be forgiven, but which does not define our character as a town.

As a former city dweller, where you feel rather anonymous amid the endless miles of suburban sprawl, I've found it inspiring and humbling to witness the simple generosity, comfort and dignity with which our townspeople respond to a death in the community. I recall someone saying once that "something always goes a bit wrong" at Meeka funerals - someone puts on the wrong CD, things don't run on time, the microphone fizzles and spits - and naturally, because it's Meekabloodytharra, we recently managed to make the national news, AGAIN, for all the wrong reasons, this one being that in all the hurly burly of his funeral preparations, Kenny was still in the morgue when his casket was buried amid a mob of grieving relatives and friends. "BURIAL BUNGLE", read the Australian news headlines. It was devastating for the family, another embarrassment for the town, and heads rolled behind the scenes for the major stuff-up - but as many locals said, Kenny himself would have laughed and laughed. He'd never been on time in his life - "late for me own funeral", as he put it - and lo and behold, he was. As many said, it was pure Meekatharra and you couldn't make it up if you tried.

But really, all I've seen is what goes right, whether it's assembling a guard of honour, fundraising to bring family members from interstate, or taking on the myriad tasks of cooking and preparation - whatever it is, people do their best with what they've got, and it comes not from the wallet and any fancy fixings, but from the heart, and from a basic, simple belief in Doing The Right Thing.

We gather together, to show respect to the deceased and to say to the living, "You are one of us; you are not alone here", and people step forward with stories that make us laugh and weep, stories full of courage, love and human frailty. Whether it's a family member, mate or neighbour, each is invited to step forward to tell part of the story of the person who has left us, and we stand and listen, remembering, sometimes smiling, holding each other and having a cry, until it is done.

And how generous of the families, in the midst of their grief, to provide the baskets of gifts that each of us can scatter in the grave - whether it's golf balls, "gold" nuggets, flower petals or balloons, we are all given the opportunity to cast them upon the one we miss as they depart on their final journey, gently blanketed by colourful symbols of a whole community's love and respect.

There are never any words that can alleviate the heart-wrenching pain felt by those who have lost someone dear to them, and in a small town like ours each loss is felt keenly throughout the community - not only on a personal level, but as a loss of part of our history, a voice silenced, a break in the tapestry that makes up our town's lifelong tale. Each of those who recently passed on was someone who contributed to Meeka in many ways, through their daily work, their family life and personal passions, and Meeka has taught me how our townsfolk recognise these contributions - not only at funerals, but in day to day life, accepting each person for who they are and appreciating what they share of themselves during their time in Meeka, whether it's a lifetime or just a few years, whether it's shaping the foundations and traditions of our town or conquering tough personal circumstances - everyone gets a fair go. And perhaps part of it all is that you think, as you release your handful of flower petals upon the coffin, "One day, it will be me." You know, deep down, you'll be brought here too, to join the silent community that perhaps stands watch, invisible hands held out in welcome as you make that last journey from the Meeka of now to the Meeka of the past, joining those who went before and waiting for those who will come. Will we join hands one hot summer's day? Will you take me along that dusty track, past the wildflowers and the mulga, and will we become ghosts in the wind, keeping watch over this vast red land?

I hope so. All of us like to think that our loved ones remain somehow, still at our sides, smiling as we try to wrestle with that unpredictable beast, Life; we hope that the end, when it comes, will be dignified, peaceful and right, and that those we lost will be waiting to carry us over, to whatever comes next.

And they are at our side, when you think about it - the roads and tracks we travel each day, the buildings we live and work in, the resources that surround us, have all been built and shaped by all of us - lifelong residents, short term visitors, ancestors, families, friends. When someone in our community passes on, we lose a whole lifetime of history, but we are richer for the innumerable contributions that will never be reported in the media, the not-so-small day to day details which make up the real Meekatharra.

The golf course, the fire brigade, a shared pizza, a freshly cut rose from the bush by the front gate, a joke at the roadhouse on a busy night, children raised, uniforms washed, sheds built, trucks fixed, a shout at the pub - these are the things that will never appear on national TV, but they're all around us, reminding us of each person's life in all its complexity and the importance of daily gratitude for what we have, brief though it might be. The old hats, dogs and utes accompanying a Meeka funeral procession are heartbreakingly familiar to us from a lifetime of use, the things we saw each day, connecting our memories so powerfully to the family member, friend, neighbour and workmate who has passed on, but is not forgotten. So we say "Thanks, mate" to our departed, and offer what comfort we can to the living as they try to move on - because we are as much a family as a town.

In Meeka, I've discovered a place where ordinary people have extraordinary stories, where you're respected for having a go, laughed at when you muck it up, given a hand when you need it - but above all a place where your contributions are recognised and remembered. They'll never show that on the national news, and perhaps the stories of those who pass on will fade away over time - but every day is an opportunity to carry on where they left off, and to celebrate the life and liveliness they brought us, because when we turn off the TV news at night, all we have is each other, and the choice to share of ourselves as best we can.

 Mum's the word

I was with my handsome personal Dr. Who plot explainer, Gary Hammer, and some fire brigade mates at the Commie the other night and we suddenly found ourselves discussing the original series of Star Trek, as you do after a drink or two on a Tuesday night in a small outback town.

When I was five years old we would be riveted to the old black and white telly every Friday evening, mesmerised by James T. Kirk and his intrepid, stylish crew. Afterwards, our dad would happily indulge us in acting out Jim's standard fight routines (a punch in the guts, followed by a karate chop to the back of the neck, then a shoulder roll into the back of the sofa/doomsday vortex) until the noise level escalated to African Buffalo Stampede levels and Mum shouted from the kitchen for us to Stop It.

Under the historic tin ceiling of the Commercial Hotel, however, adult logic reared its ugly head. How come, no matter where they beamed down, they would always run into someone in charge, handy to a nearby headquarters? This wouldn't happen in real life. In reality, they would land somewhere like outer Mandurah and be greeted by the alien equivalent of Craig and maybe a few of Craig's mates. "This ere's Bazza, Wazza, Chimp and Crusty," Craig would say. "And this is me Holden what we're tryin' ter get Davo's old 352 into. Yer got any smokes mate?" The Star Trek crew would then end up in some sort of tangle with Centrelink, like an interstellar episode of Housos.

As more beer was consumed, more questions arose. Why in God's name did they keep using the Transporter, which was clearly unreliable, breaking down in nearly every episode? Why did blokes keep signing up to be the guys in the red security outfits, when none of them ever survived through an entire episode? Why did they never take spare dilithium crystals, always running out of them millions of light years from the nearest Star Bunnings? Why on earth did they keep letting Kirk beam down to planets full of slinky, scantily-clad glamazon alien women when he had a proven track record of thinking with his dick and nearly getting everyone killed? Why did the initial scouting parties always consist of the most important leaders of the crew, leaving only Chekov and Nurse Christine in charge?

As we marveled at these absurd illogicalities, I realised what the problem was: <u>there was no mum</u>. You know, someone with common sense. For example, they were always beaming down to some godforsaken unknown planet with only a tricorder and a few phasers, which never worked against whatever slimy awful thing they encountered there. No sandwiches, no bottled water, not even a spare jumper. No mum in the universe would have let this go on. "James, have you got your warm jacket? Where's Scotty's lunch box? Uhura, you are NOT going out dressed like that, put something sensible on."

So, when you think about it, Star Trek was the galactic equivalent of letting Dad take the kids camping. You know what I mean - sure, it's awesome fun, and you learn heaps of cool stuff but unfortunately a lot of dads aren't always on top of things such as realising that you've been wearing your Spiderman costume for 12 days and nights straight and the filth-encrusted polyester fabric has actually melded into your top skin layers and may need to be surgically removed, or noticing that your little brother and the dog have been living on peanut butter and sugar from the same dish while your older brother has been playing Angry Birds for 157 hours and is now unable to blink or speak. "Dad, can me and Pete play with the gun?" you ask. "Sure," says Dad, preoccupied with re-wiring the boat motor that Mum told him to get fixed last summer but then his mate Kev came round and they drank beer and started fooling around with the quad bike instead and now that doesn't work either.

Mums stop us from turning into Lord Of The Flies. We should have official mums allocated around the world make sure countries get a grip on themselves. Groups of emergency mums could be sent to global hot zones to sort things out. They wouldn't need weapons. "No telly until that mess is cleaned up!" Imagine, if we had more mums in charge, how we could cut down on all the excessive occupational health and safety madness, overloaded court systems and so on - "Stop that or you'll poke someone's eye out!" "I don't care who did it, you're all going to your rooms until you've learned how to behave."

It was wonderfully exciting to imagine myself taking part in the gripping, life-or-death adventures of the Star Trek crew, but in reality I know that if I ever did have to venture on to an alien planet swarming with huge carnivorous plants and six-eyed bug monsters, I would definitely want a spare sandwich, and my mum. Gary would be handy too, but I'm not 100% sure how he'd go around the scantily-clad women - he might need me to rescue him. If the transporter's working, that is. Would you like to go first? I just need to go get my jumper.

booty scooterin'

Something I like about Meeka - and perhaps it's true of most small towns - is that you really can just be yourself. In the city, people dress or act differently in order to distinguish themselves from the crowd, but Meeka is the kind of place where you can happily go to the shop in your pyjamas, Batman costume, bathers or just your bare socks (and, during one entertaining night at the roadhouse, a purple dragon onesie) because that's what you happened to have on when you realised you desperately needed a one-kilo bag of minties and seventeen energy drinks. Even if you decide to run down Main Street without any clothes on, as Naked Man did the other week, the road trains will patiently wait until you're done and someone will make sure you get home safe and sound to your underwear. This is why I feel completely comfortable with my sudden mid-life scooter ~~crisis~~ hobby.

I had no intention of getting a scooter. Oh, I've done my bikie time in years gone by, cruising the highways on a dodgily-modified old Kawasaki 750 LTD, and there is also the fact that my handsome personal high-speed corner-slide instructor Gary Hammer cuts quite a dashing figure in a set of leathers, but as a middle aged lady of a certain girth I felt that my two-wheeled days were behind me. Then Les gave me his old prospecting scooter. "Dunno how long it'll last," he said.

It lasted long enough (about 4 hours and 33 minutes) for me to become addicted. So were the dogs. With all three of them perched in the footwell at the same time, tongues flapping and Red Dog standing with his front paws on the handlebars, we looked like something from a not very good circus, or an accident looking for somewhere to happen. I put the urgent engine repairs on the back burner while I ordered more important items such as vintage flying gloves, and matching goggles for the dogs.

It was like riding around in a comfortable office chair. The world was our oyster! Well, the world for a 3 kilometre radius, which seemed to be the limit of the poor old scooter's tired carburetor. As the various nasty mechanical noises increased Gary said, "Don't ride it anymore until I've had a look at the engine" but of course I didn't listen and an hour later I arrived home very hot and embarrassed, pushing the dead scooter along the dusty track to our beloved bush hovel. "I told you so," said Gaz in a suspiciously satisfied tone of voice as I added the scooter to our pile of Things That Need Fixing And No You Can't Have That We're Gunna Do It Up One Day. The dogs went and sat hopefully on its silent corpse and I got on the internet.

A couple of weeks later Roy Wybenga turned up with my new old scooter on the back of his truck. The red and cream paint job glowed gloriously in the sunset, and the whipper-snipper growl of its 49cc's of raw power filled the air with promises of adventure and wild times on the road. I set off with Honey the foxy-chihuahua on board, braced safely between my boots and wearing her glamorous new red dog goggles.

"It's the Meeka Mosquito!" exclaimed Steve at the corner store. "You look like one of those eccentric characters that ride around Paris," said Timika. "Who's the crazy lady on the circus bike?" asked the tourists at the food van. I hooned around town at the scooter's impressive top speed of forty three and a half kilometres an hour, the wind almost blowing through my hair, Honey peering happily through her goggles, kids cheering as we whizzed past. At least I think they were cheering. Maybe they were laughing, or possibly throwing rocks. It was hard to tell through my extremely stylish vintage goggles, which kept fogging up from the heat of my menopausal forehead. I knew I didn't really look cool - but I didn't care. In my mind's eye, I was slim, dashing, maybe a little bit dangerous, an outback Emma Peel on wheels, the scooter and I as one, woman and machine, road rebels, free and wild.

This exhilarating delusion lasted all the way to the roadhouse, where the dog and I were asked to pose for a photo. Somewhere in the USA, a family is probably sitting through a laptop slide show right now looking at a photo of me and Honey, parked out the front of the roadhouse in our goggles. "Check out the clown lady and her pet rat I saw in the Austrian outerback," I imagine the cheerful tourist man saying to his startled neighbours.

Now, I know you bloke readers will be asking yourselves, "Yeah, but what about the tech specs and fuel consumption?" Here are some quick facts:

Scooters are basically made out of some tin cans, recycled Barbie doll plastic and elastic bands. I think they also have some electricity in them. Or something. Anyway, they don't use much fuel. Meekatharra is about 500 metres long on an average weekday, and our camp is about 3 km from the Wiluna turnoff unless you take the old haulpack track and cut behind Elaine's house and go past the quartz blow, which reduces the fuel consumption by about a furlong, but if Red Dog has escaped from the bush camp and you have to turn around and take him back, the idiot, this of course increases the fuel consumption by 1.3 dogs per metre, or, in layperson's terms, about five dollars a week unless Gaz and the boys have been doing wheelies on it behind the fire station, in which case it will be broken. Of course you should add in your handbag wind resistance ratios, but you get the general idea: if you can handle the laughter and abuse, it's an economical way to get about, and you can load a surprising number of things on to a scooter, such as your weekly shopping or a small family.

As an indication of just how hilariously embarrassing my scooter looks, here is an amazing fact: no one has tried to steal it. This could be a record in Meeka, where the only sure way to protect your motorbike from thieves is to chain it to a trained attack panther armed with a backpack armalite heat-sensor rifle. And that's just while you pop into the chemist. It looks like something Minnie Mouse would own; the words "impressive", "powerful" and "dignified" do not come to mind. "You kids stop trying to put coins in that scooter, it's not a ride," said Tanja during our afternoon shift at the roadhouse. Miners On Bikes stopped in for petrol on their big Harleys and laughed at it; I'm pretty sure I saw it cringe, and went out to reassure it. "They're just jealous," I whispered. At least I wasn't riding around in my pyjamas.

Now, in a small town, daily existence often descends into mayhem, because everyone knows each other, and anything you say or do takes on a comical life of its own amid the rumour mill and not-always-quite-accurate pool of communal knowledge, so naturally it wasn't long before my scooter quickly led to various social misadventures.

One afternoon Chad, one of our local coppers, came in and said something about a scooter. I should explain to any non-local readers at this point that our local fence builder's nickname is Scoota, and I was looking for him to come and fix our fence, which had been blown down by the Christmas willy-willy; also, the words "Scoota" and "scooter" are almost indistinguishable in Australian (try to keep up, OK?). In addition, Jo was looking for me to give her lessons on her new scooter, Tom and Judy were talking about getting scooters, Roy was on his way to deliver my new old scooter, and I was also waiting for parts from Perth for the old old scooter which Gary, after a few drinks at the Commie, had promised to fix up and give to Nigel, who had not at any time ever expressed any interest in having one.

It's hard to describe the horrendously confusing conversation that took place as Chad tried to explain that his scooter was for sale. "I hear you're looking for a scooter." "Yeah, have you seen him?" "Who?" "Scoota." "Yeah, I'm asking $1800." "1800? To fix a fence?" "What? No, for the scooter." "No, Roy's picking it up, it's just $800." "No, my scooter." "Roy's picking up a scooter for you too?" "Who?" This went on until even the customers at the back of the queue needed a Bex and a lie down.

Then there was the roadhouse toilet key incident. One of the truckies had wandered off with the key to number 4; rather than waste time walking around the huge truck parking area in the dark, I hopped on to the scooter with my safety vest and torch. I spotted the truckie over by the creek-side parking area.

"Oi, have you got the key to the loo?" I yelled. He looked at me, startled - he had misheard my question as a phrase involving the words "me" and "root" (an Australian word for sexual intercourse). He shook his head vehemently and waved me away. "No, no!" "Yes, yes!" I yelled back, pointing at him, making a "give it to me" gesture. He began to panic, and wound down the truck window. "Nah I'm right love," he called out. "The key!" I yelled. "The loo key!" "Oh! The LOO key! Crikey love I thought you was offerin' yer services!"

Now, I know it gets lonely on the highways but I never thought that a wombat-shaped, irritable middle-aged lady wearing a safety vest and riding a tiny scooter could be interpreted as canvassing for clandestine entertainment activities - but there you go. I considered trying it out on Gaz for a bit of frisky safety vest fun at home, but realised it would never compete with the thrill of our good old Dance Of The Seven Tea Towels (Gaz is quite light on his feet, with the right music).

Anyway, the little scooter found its moment of glory when I decided to make a spectacle of myself in our charming town parade, leading the fire brigade in my firefighting clobber, with Honey perched on the handlebars in a home-made firefighter helmet. Ahead of us were 20-odd members of the Vietnam vets' motorcycle club. My scooter would easily have fit into any one of their Harley panniers. The cost of decorating the scooter with emergency services tape, a flashing helmet light and a small dog: my dignity. The look on 24 big burly bikie blokes' faces as I came around the corner: priceless.

There have been many adventures on the little scooter, and I'm sure there will be more to come - it's a wonderful reminder that life can surprise and delight you at any age, and that a little outback town can be a place where you're free to be who you need to be. All I ask fellas, is, please, if you see me riding along in my safety vest, do try to hold yourselves back.

if you're still alive in the morning can you get me an icy pole ?

We've been in bed for ages. A week? What year is it? I think we're up and about now, but I'm absolutely off my face on prescription codeine and cough syrup, so this might all be a dream. We have The Cough - you know the one. You have it. We have it. Everyone who comes into the roadhouse has it. We keep passing it around, like a borrowed lawn mower. Once we're finished with it, you can have it back. I'm sorry we took it for so long.

It hit us late one night. I was dozing off when my handsome personal Vicks chest rub attendant, Gary Hammer, began to make terrible wheezing noises. Then he started coughing, then retching, then clutching at his chest. "I'm taking you to the hospital!" I declared. "Nah, I'll be right," he said, being a typical bloke, except that through the phlegm it sounded like "naCCCHgaabeHARRGHightFLURFPPHGH." I speak fluent Bloke so I just gave him some cool water and lay there listening to his lurching, gargled breathing, hoping he wouldn't die during the night. Who would do the genny fuel filter changes?

After a few hours, I began to cough as well, with a throat that felt like razor blades. Soon both of us were thrashing helplessly in retching, choking coughing fits. I somehow got out of bed and went into town to buy 37 icy poles, heaps of flu tablets and all the chicken noodle soup I could carry (2).

I think it was me who drove into town. I'm not sure. It might have been the dog. By now I couldn't talk and had to make myself understood with sign language and choking noises. Even the chemist backed away.

When I got home, Gaz sounded worse. If he'd been a horse I would've shot him. Poor Gary! A firm pillow over the face would have put him out of his misery, but I was unable to move, gripped by the coughing seizures racking my feverish body. "We'll go to the doctor Who in the whirlygig noodle pole," I moaned, then passed out. We lay curled in bed for days, coughing and deranged, the dogs whining anxiously at the door. "Just eat the cat," I whispered. "Tell Lassie to get help. Good boy."

Anyway, the only reason we got up was because the Bathurst 1000 was on the telly. Gaz crawled to the sofa and somehow found the herculean strength to operate the remote control. I could tell that he was delirious because he began excitedly croaking on about someone called Craig and the 0.00001 of a second difference a set of kryptonite tyres could make. I dragged my aching, 2000-kilo jellified body to the recliner chair, and after half an hour's rest I was able to raise my 30-pound eyelids and stare blankly at the cars going round and round and round and ohhhhh BLUUURGH. It could have been Portuguese Llama Fighting for all I cared, and I didn't, because all I could do was cough and gaze weakly at the dogs eating my lung chunks off the floor. I was so out of it that apparently I agreed to book us a holiday at next year's Bathurst 1000; I don't have any interest in motor sports, so this was the equivalent of booking a bloke into a four-day National Tampon Conference. I hauled us both to the doctor before things could get worse.

We seem to be better, but now Ebola is lurking on the horizon. When it comes to Meeka, it will arrive at the roadhouse, where we spread good cheer and five dollar notes seething with unspeakably hideous public bacteria. The Cough pops into the roadhouse regularly, and I can imagine it making good friends with Ebola, which likes to party, or as they say scientifically, "mutate".

The reason we know that Ebola is coming is because of the officials on the telly. You know what I mean - we all watch the movies, we know how it works. First there's a few rogue cases which get the human interest segments on the news, then it gets a little more serious and people in suits have press conferences on national TV where they say things like "We have strict protocols in place" and "Our medical experts have everything under control." Are they kidding? Haven't they watched Contagion? We all know someone's unregistered pet monkey will escape and spread it to some illegal dockside workers. Then it will mutate via a forgotten underground sewage system and a low-ranking government whistleblower will reveal that the bulk supplies of public medical masks are just cheap Chinese swimming goggles because of budget cuts. As soon as we heard the phrase "There is no need for concern about ebola in the western world", Gaz and I looked at each other and said, "We're all gonna die!!"

So don't worry about The Cough, because I suspect that it's not going to be a problem for much longer. Just stay in bed and keep gargling down that cough syrup, and if you see our dog driving the car, can you ask him to get us some more icy poles?

a long time ago in a shed far far away

We could have it running in a weekend or two I reckon

Easy

Don't ask Harvey about that old Chevy at Sherwood. Don't bother about Gary's '78 Kingswood either. And forget about that old jailbar Ford of Norm's. You can't have it. Many have tried. You'll have a go one day yourself. Maybe you already have. Do you lie awake at night, thinking about it? What about that Leyland out the back of wherever it was off the Pingandy track? Too far to get. Unless you can borrow Greg's truck. Except Dan's using it. Hope the bastard isn't after that 1940's Jeep carcass on the Wiluna road that whatsisname's mate's mate told you about at the pub. Or was it a Bedford, on the Mt. Clere road? Never mind. It's not there. It doesn't exist, except in your mind. But the siren call of old broken cars calls you and calls you. Every time you come across some lovely rusting wreck in the bush you ask around and you find the old bloke who reckons he owns it and you hem and haw and ask him what he'd take for it.

"Yer can't ave it," he says. "I'm gunna do it up one day."

It could be every outback bloke's nickname. Gunna. The quad bikes, the dirt bikes, the cars, the gennies - "it's in good nick except for the starter motor and a few hoses, it'd just take a weekend to get er goin again." But it never takes just a weekend. It takes decades. It takes a lifetime. It never ends. You promise yourself you'll go see Adam about getting the compressor off that old Landy. Nathan's bound to have some spare aircon hose out at Sherwood. The missus rolls her eyes and orders parts on the internet. They sit in boxes next to the dog bed and the broken weed whacker and the bucket of bent tek screws you found at the tip and that three-legged table you're going to fix as soon as you get round to it. After a while there's a broken Honda genset motor sitting on top of the parts boxes and then some dieselly rags and the mice get into it and then it's too hot and you wander off to help Tony put the roof on his new shed, during which you come up with a grouse idea for a way to build a 12 volt airconditioner out of the fan kit from that out-of-rego Ford that Matt left behind, but while you're fossicking around for the bag of wiring connectors you swear you left on the work bench, Mark comes round and gives you a hand with the solenoid on the genny, and then you both go have a look at the tip for the KTM frame Richard thought he saw yesterday and crikey where's the day gone?

You could buy an old resto on Gumtree for the price of a paycheque or two. But it's not the same. You want the derelict beauty you found sleeping in the timeless ravaging outback, the thrill of poking about until you find some clue to the year model and you can't believe your eyes. It's got a straight 8! They stopped making those in the 1930's! This thing could be worth thousands! If you could get it out of the bush. If you could borrow a truck. If the station owner would let you have it. But you can't have it. Never mind that it's got an actual tree growing through the engine bay - he's gunna fix it up. Never mind how you'd explain it to the missus. At least it would be too big for her to chuck in the bin. Unless she had help. But you don't think like that. You just see the machine. You want it. But you can't have it. Because the other bloke is gunna . . . You laugh. You shake your head. He's full of it! But you'd do it up. For sure. Maybe next year. After you finish the Valiant. It only needs a new alternator and rewiring and the front end doing and a decent set of rims and it'll be good as - What? What's she carrying on about this time? "Get those filthy engine thingamajiggies off the coffee table! NOW! Yer tea's ready."

So you scrub the oil off your hands in the laundry sink, eat your dinner and watch the news, the alien and strange soft people from the city who you meet only when their things break and they bring them to you, rushed, annoyed and perhaps just that little bit up 'emselves because they finished high school or went to uni, trying to talk all blokey in their clean clothes and brand new Kathmandu hiking boots.

On Friday nights you sit among the ragged semi-circle of blokes in the Commie beer garden and listen to the tantalising rumours of sheds, stations and dimly-remembered treasures glimpsed last month, or last year, or back in the eighties, by a mate, or his mate, or a mate's dad's pop . . . an Ariel 250 side-valve . . . a Bedford flatbed chassis . . . a Puch...or Lambretta? ...hanging from the ceiling . . . pretty sure it was a Valiant two-door . . . said he knew a bloke who knew where there's a Matchless, untouched . . . wouldn't sell it to me . . . looked like part of an Indian Chief V-twin . . . behind the old pump shed . . . some station past Mt. Augustus, can't remember the name of it now . . .

I sit at the ladies' table and watch Gary's eyes grow distant. I used to wonder what he loves about these old wrecks, all the flotsam and jetsam of Meeka's tough, hot past, things that have broken down, as sad as worn-out horses, caked with red dirt, their tales lost in the silent bush. But I see the way he looks when he talks about them, how all the blokes go quiet and dreamy as the stories drift away into the soft outback night, their inner vision carrying them along in the vehicles of yesteryear, all the broken, lonely machines that one day . . . one day . . . could rise again. Waiting for a bloke to come along.

So we find ourselves listening to some skin-cancered, faded-eyed old station bloke in his work-ragged lifelong Akubra, not too busy to spare some time for us, the odd couple in our battered Landcruiser wondering if it's OK to have a look around his tip. Because there's something personal about a bloke's tip, and it doesn't seem right to just go fossicking around without asking.

"That was me pop's first truck, we used ter picnic down ter the Granites, all the kids in the back. Drove Nan ter the hospital durin the floods with the poor baby that never got a name, buried out by the big gidgee if yer go have a look. Did the mail route. Did the musterin. Pop gave er ter dad an dad gave er ter me, drove it inter Meekatharra every Sat'day until I met the missus. Kids used it as a paddock basher til they moved off to the city. Old girl's bin sittin ere ever since."

So we gaze at the "old girl" amid the grass-grown, hard-baked soil, and I finally understand that the crumbling bodies lined up in the scrub aren't rubbish at all - they're a timeline in steel, as poignant as a photo album, each one a milestone in a bloke's life. The first one. The one he got off a mate. The one that hit the bullock. The truck. The ute. One for the young bloke to learn on. The bush basher. A dozen dead mustering bikes. From a time when a man and a car could understand each other, when it was hands on and you did it yourself and it worked and you got on with things.

Swearing and sweating. Bruised, cut knuckles. Exhaust burns. Oil and dirt. No RAC, no diagnostic tools, no computers, no mobile phone, no downloaded workshop manual, just the knowledge in your head and whatever tools you had ready to hand. All the bikes, cars, gennies and trucks, fixed over and over again, stripped down to essentials, making do with fencing wire, cloth-plugged tyres, home-made sealant - more intimate than anything experienced with a woman, your hands recalling every awkward bastard fuel line or exhaust clamp, the years and years of bush tracks like the back of your hand, full of places where you cracked a sump, holed a tyre, felt the diff go, snapped a leaf spring . . .

"They built em tough back then," he says. "Go anywhere. Probably start no worries if yer chucked a new battery in er."

"Would you be interested in selling it?" asks Gaz.

The old bloke looks off at the horizon with a frown.

I share a secret, sympathetic smile with Gary. We know what's coming next. Because an old truck is time spent with dad, with pop, with sons and brothers and mates; it's had a taste of you, and its oil and rust are in your blood. You'll never do it up, because that would be like wishing the dead back to life, and you know that when you drive the corrugated station tracks the ghosts of men and trucks follow behind you, generations of long-gone cattle dogs in the back, the laughter of your children fading in the bush, the voice of your missus calling high and thin from the back of the house, the rough touch of a dozen good dogs who broke your heart, but you can't put all that into words, it's too big, buried so deep and strong.

So the old bloke says what he needs to say to keep the hard-earned years where he can see them, burnt by the sun, rusting in the red dust wind, in the place they belong.

"Nah, yer can't ave it," he says. "I'm gunna do er up."

And so we shake his hand, and we walk away.

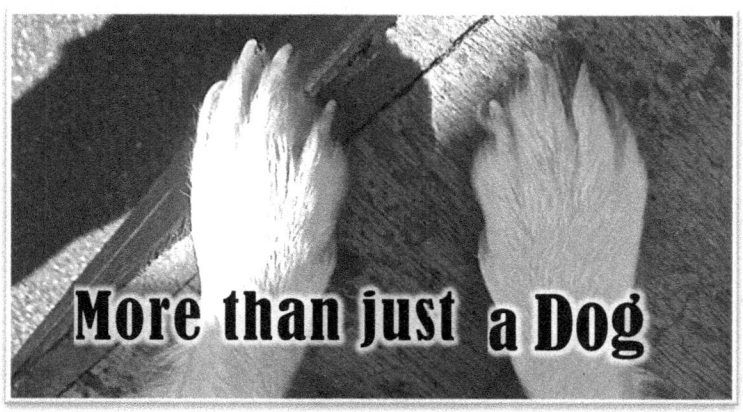

More than just a Dog

This year we kicked off the Christmas holiday season on our hands and knees in the dirt of our driveway, sobbing over the bodies of our poisoned dogs. If you've ever seen a dog go down with bait poisoning, you know what a miserable, ugly thing it is. Honey gagged and cried, her head arched so far back that I thought her neck would break. Sophie howled and howled, slamming herself against the solid fence until she finally fell down dead, her beautiful kelpie face lacerated and smeared with blood from the blows. I hear the sound over and over in my mind. I never want to hear anything like that again.

The nearest veterinarian is 450 kilometres from Meeka. There wasn't even time to get a gun - and trust me, if you see a dog go down with a poison bait, especially strychnine, you'll know straightaway what I mean when I say that a bullet would be a kindness. I won't go into any more details. You'll be sick, and I can't think about it.

After Honey went down, our friend Paul - one of us must have called him, asking if he could find someone with a gun, but I can't remember - found Red Dog outside our compound fence, cold and rigid, his mouth gaping open from his frantic struggle to breathe. He died twenty yards from our bed as we lay sleeping.

As we tried to get our heads around finding Red Dog, Sophie

suddenly began howling and convulsing. I couldn't go to her, in case she bit me with her poisoned mouth. I sank to my knees and leaned against the screen door with my eyes clenched shut, feeling it every time she drove her head into the compound wall. She was dead three minutes later. And there we stood, in shock, with our entire beloved dog family lying dead all around us.

We try to comfort ourselves with the thought that it was relatively quick. I don't know if it felt quick to the dogs. It probably felt like forever. I imagine it felt agonising, bewildering and awful. I know that's how it felt to us. We can handle road crash rescues, fires and first aid, but those three dogs were the heart of our family, so you can imagine just how well we coped after one dog after another went down convulsing and crying in front of our eyes.

The horrendous experience didn't stop there. Gary got sick just from handling Red Dog. He's still sick now. He rolled a cigarette, and that's all it took. As for me, my guardian angel deserves a medal, because somehow, in spite of having both hands covered in dog vomit and saliva from trying to help Honey, I didn't touch my face, wiping my tears with the back of my arm. If I'd touched my face with my hands, there's a good chance I'd be dead too. Because strychnine never sleeps. Once it's out there, it's out there forever, toxic, waiting for the next creature to ingest it and die in agony.

We know it was strychnine. And we're prepared to say it's our own fault, for letting the dogs out of our fenced compound. The racecourse horses are all on summer holiday, so we didn't worry about the dogs having the run of the place, and Red Dog was doing a pretty good job flushing out rabbits and chasing off the feral town dogs who, for reasons that remain a mystery to all of us, are never picked up by the animal ranger and who do so much damage to livestock and domestic animals, to the point where locals are afraid to walk their dogs down the street in their own neighbourhood. It never, ever occurred to us that there would be anything poisonous around a public recreation area so close to town, a place where visiting horses, dogs and children all come to stay and play and rest up as they follow the WA rodeo circuit.

But maybe Red Dog went somewhere he shouldn't have, and maybe he ate something meant for feral animals. But Honey, my tiny companion of ten years, and Sophie, our goofy young kelpie, were harmless home dogs and didn't deserve to die, let alone in such a rotten, cruel way. Gary and I, who try to do our bit around town with the fire brigade and general helping out, didn't deserve to be smeared with deadly poison on our hands and faces, with Gaz losing work from the strychnine cramps - even now, six weeks later, he still hasn't entirely come good from it, and we don't know what the long term effects might be.

We're perplexed, because baiting is done many kilometres away, and Red Dog was always within earshot - he always came running up within a minute or two when we whistled him. Did he go farther away that morning? The thing is, you see, that strychnine works fast. We'll never know. We don't want to think it was deliberate. We don't want to wonder who, or what, or why, or how. We don't know what to think. We don't know what to do.

"It's the crows, they eat the baits, then poo it out," people said. But ours aren't the only dogs in town to die from what looks like poisoning in the last few weeks. And if that many crows are dropping toxic poo around town, shouldn't we be worried? Shouldn't we be totally freaking out? Because maybe next time it won't be a dog.

My four year old nephew was here not so long ago. We took him walking all over the racecourse area and the bush around town. "Pick up anything that looks interesting, Sam!" we encouraged. "You might find some gold, or an old bottle!" Or a poisonous bit of dirt. Or a dried crow dropping that looks like an unusual rock, shot through with strychnine. You might get it on your little fingers, Sam, without even knowing it, while we egg you on to explore and not be afraid of nature, and you might go digging around in the dirt because this month you are a Pirate and that's what pirates do, they dig for gold, and then you might put your fingers in your mouth or in your eyes or up your nose, because you get sweaty and grubby and snotty and you're four years old and that's what little kids do.

I didn't grow up in the outback, but I'm not some tenderfoot city fool

- I grew up rural, we raised animals for food, and I learned from a young age how to care for and kill livestock to put on the plate. I've helped with roo and rabbit shooting. I've seen what wild dogs can do to sheep and cattle. I completely get it that feral animals are a problem in Australia to an extent that doesn't generally occur anywhere else in the world, and Gary and I both understand how and why 1080 and strychnine are still used in rural Australia and in New Zealand, even though every other country in the world deems them to be inhumane and has banned them. We both understand the sheer bloody hard work required to get our steaks on to the supermarket shelf.

But what's the price of these poisons? When you do a bit of research you discover that countless numbers of indigenous and domestic animals are killed - often in terrible, drawn-out agony - as a result of directly or indirectly ingesting bait materials. Tourists' dogs, people's horses, and even working dogs, as in the terrible, terrible case in Queensland where a group of mustering blokes lost all of their cattle dogs in one morning because the adjoining station manager had baited the shared stockyard - and didn't tell them.

We feel like our home has been poisoned. We feel like our hearts and thoughts have been poisoned. I don't feel the same when I visit the shops, when I look around at the people in my adopted community. Was it you? I think as I force a smile. Was it someone you know? Do you know and you're not telling? Did you do it to us, or just anyone, or what? Was it an accident? Will it happen again? And then my final question, echoing in my mind each day: What if next time, it's a child?

People in Meeka were incredibly kind when they heard our terrible news, and that may be the one thing that stopped us from getting in the car and just driving away. People I barely know came up with tears in their eyes and hugged me at the roadhouse and the shops. We've been offered the first pick of so many puppies, offers of dogs and heartfelt sympathy - I can't begin to tell you all what that means to both of us. It has been a great balm to our sorrow, and reminded us why we chose to live here in the first place.

We're okay now. Sort of. We get up and go to work, do the shopping, take the rubbish to the tip. We do our bit with the fire brigade and share a drink and a laugh at the pub. But no one sees us curled up together on our bed, sobbing into each other's shoulders because the dog beds are empty and there's this awful silence when we come home from work. No one hears me when I just drop the wheelbarrow and sit on the track howling like a five year old when I come across a fading set of Honey's cock-eyed paw prints and I remember the years I spent with that brave little dog who would not let me leave her at home, who insisted on coming sea kayaking, scooter riding, bicycle touring and even snorkeling, standing on my back as we explored the rock pools of Port Phillip Bay. She even put up with wearing a tiny fire helmet and riding on the "firefighting" scooter in the Meekatharra Parade, and she loved Gary so much that her barking turned to earpiercing squeaks, whether he'd been out in the genny shed for five minutes or away from home for three days. She was my shadow, my buddy, my heart.

Gaz and I try to focus on the good memories - the joy they brought us, the good times they had while they were here. Red Dog, who just wanted to be a good boy and ride on the scooter all day. Sophie, who liked to joke and tease, curled up in a farting, snoring tangle with Red Dog in the bucket bed that was too small for the pair of them. Honey, smart, cheeky and so trusting, a well-known little mate on Melbourne film shoots, always at my side through thick and thin, sturdily soldiering on through all our adventures.

Those of us who have lost dogs to poison know that it's not just about the dogs. It poisons our sense of safety, our confidence in the community. It casts a shadow over how we see our neighbours, our town. The landscape is suddenly transformed, no longer so beautiful and beckoning. It affects your desire to take part, to help, to contribute.

Will we ever share our lives with another dog? Yes - because we can't imagine going through life without them. A dog reminds you that life's not so serious, that sometimes it's good to just roll in the dirt, bark at the bowerbirds and make a fool of yourself in the swimming pool. They want so little, and they give so much; there is no heart more generous, more forgiving, than the heart of a dog.

We know we'll never find out who, or how, or why, and we're not the type of people to go around looking for payback; it would be a dishonour to our dogs, who forgave and loved no matter what. So we'll move on, and we'll keep doing what we do, going to work, fighting fires, helping our mates and being a part of this town. But maybe you'll see in our eyes, once in a while, that part of us is gone, hidden, broken, withdrawn - because our family has been poisoned, our adopted town has been poisoned, and deep down, I don't know if we'll ever feel the same about it again.

Clockwise from top

Sophie 2014 - 2015

Red Dog 2013 - 2015

Honey 2004 - 2015

Intermission: Some Meeka Moments

Meekatharra - a busy regional hub

Mad prospectors wander in from time to time, crazed with gold fever

Expect the unexpected

Every Christmas morning Santa and the Commercical Hotel elves hand out lollies from the old fire truck. Santa's identity is a closely-guarded secret in Meekatharra.

All in it together: the annual town foctrace at the racecourse - even the town doctor took part last year

There's always time to stop and chat - Marty & Gary enjoy a roadside chin-wag during the floods

Big trucks carrying even bigger trucks - road trains and heavy haulage are a daily sight in Meeka

Me, Gary and our volunteer fire brigade mates all scrubbed up for our annual photo

If there's a ute, it's compulsory for blokes to gather round the back of it

Far left: Gary & Kim prove you're accepted for who you are in Meeka

Left, Gary & Missy cool off at Five Mile mine pit

Left, Janine Mongoo, one of our national rodeo champions; above, the quintessential Aussie ute & swag

Right: growing up in the outback: Meeka kids with their bush bicycles, at home in their traditional landscape

Below: locals aren't fazed by wet season floods

Bottom right: Russell holds back Bindie, the ferocious post office guard dog

fifty shades of HOT

Are the kids a bit bored now that Christmas is over and we're in the middle of a heatwave? Why not bring them for a visit to Gaz 'n' Anna's Krazy Kritter Kingdom for a day of nature fun? You'll be amazed at the variety of wildlife hiding out from the broiling sun. Check out Barry The Bathroom Bungarra! Run screaming as he stands at his full five foot height from his perch on the washing machine, hissing and waving his claws! Take a stroll through Gwarda Garden, where all your snake nightmares come true! Will you survive a trip to Terror Toilet, leaping over angry scorpions, then peeling plague-like numbers of frogs from your nether regions while avoiding the cranky brown snake cooling off next to the cistern? Test your courage in the Shower of Screams - is that an enormous millipede tangled in your hair, or just an excited stick insect? Remember, there's some things that Mortein just can't kill - and you're probably sleeping next to a whole nest of 'em! Kids will love our "dead mouse water balloons" - when it's fifty degrees, they just swell up in no time and it's stinky slingshot fun for everyone! That's right - Gaz 'n' Anna's Krazy Kritter Kingdom, fun for the whole family! Don't forget your epi-pen!

But you probably don't want to visit - after all, it's the same at your house, isn't it? With Meeka temperatures soaring, just about everyone's place has turned into an emergency Noah's Ark, with lizards, birds, insects and things you've never seen before, all desperate for any shade or water. It reached 50 at our place - at least, that's what our thermometer said, but it only goes up to 50 (!!). I realise the airport weather station says our high was 47.6 or something, but where are they keeping their thermometer, in the fridge? The road crew came into the roadhouse one afternoon and said they measured 73 - yes, SEVENTY THREE - Celsius on the bitumen up towards Karalundi. And they think forty's hot in the city!

When I came home I discovered that my handsome personal 12-volt air conditioner inventor, Gary Hammer, had put a wading pool in the living room. It was lovely, sitting in the lounge pool with our new dog, Missy, who is a part bull-arab, part giraffe we adopted from Geraldton. Gary had thoughtfully placed the pool so that we could watch TV or fall into it while trying to get out of bed in the middle of the night (we live in one room due to the fact that 95 percent of our home is filled with motorcycle carcasses, half-built engines, ancient steam generators and helicopter parts. I think we had a separate bedroom once but I haven't seen it for a couple of years.)

We worried briefly that the indoor pool would attract snakes, but as I pointed out, the snakes all appeared to be living in the house anyway so why worry about it. Only a couple of nights earlier, I'd felt something tickling my ankle while I was doing the dishes in my bare feet. I thought it was just one of the wretched frogs, and kept kicking it away. Then I looked down. Oops! Sorry about kicking you in the head Mr. Snake! It was just a bandy-bandy, a sort-of-harmless banded desert snake, but I'd warned it months ago not to cross the line from the tool area to the living area and it didn't listen and so it had to face the consequences ("Oh god Gary hit it with your boot hit it with your boot QUICK AAAGHH") of its poor decision-making skills, part of the harsh code of survival and housework in the outback. The big black-and-yellow gwarda in the breezeway and the pretty but deadly olive-coloured dugite behind the rubbish cage both escaped - I nearly stepped on each of them, but fortunately both snakes were very considerate and moved quickly to get out of my way.

Anyway, the pool came with a bonus plastic wind-up shark toy. The dog was fascinated by it, and sat rigidly staring to see if it would move again. At two in the morning, when I got up to fight my way past the scorpions to our charming outdoor toilet, she was still there, staring at the shark in the dark. "It's not going to do anything," I whispered. "Go to bed." She looked at me briefly. *But it might*, she seemed to be saying. *I'm just making sure.* She was still staring when I went back to sleep. "Well, at least we're not going to be attacked in the night by a plastic shark," I thought to myself as I slapped a couple of stink beetles out of my hair and drifted off to the relaxing sound of The Thing That Makes That Noise In The Wall No It's Not The Cat He's On Top Of The Fridge. "Something just bit me on the back," moaned Gaz. "Just roll on to it and squash it," I said comfortingly. "Try not to make it angry."

The highlight of the heatwave was the night a tiny microbat collapsed in the living room at Gary's feet. He picked it up, and it was still alive. "What do we do with it?" we wondered. I quickly googled "heat stressed bat" and - how I love the internet - there were instructions! We followed them to the letter, holding the little bat up to a dish of water, which it gratefully began lapping at with its tiny pink tongue, then we carefully stretched its wings open and sprayed them with water. We put it in a makeshift little "bat cave" made from a garden basket and a wet tea towel, and it revived, soon disappearing into the night. We were delighted for days, wondering how our tiny bat friend was going, our hearts warmed by our little "Born Free" encounter, until we found its dried-up corpse clinging to the inside of my motorcycle helmet, where it had crawled from its rescue basket to die the night we "saved" it. "Let's pretend it lived and flew away," I said to Gaz as we gently dropped its tiny little body in the bin.

The bungarra on the washing machine was a whole different story. I don't know what it was doing in the laundry shed ("hmm, delicates or standard cycle?") but I must have given it a fright because there was this unearthly crashing and banging, and I looked in the doorway to see this enormous startled lizard standing on the washing machine, clinging to the window. I backed away. When I first moved to Australia, my wedding present from my mother-in-law was a large coffee-table photo book emblazoned with large red letters saying "AUSTRALIA - THESE CREATURES CAN BITE AND KILL!". I think there was a photo of my mother-in-law on page one. The book contained melodramatic warnings about bungarras and perenties, with phrases like "these deadly prehistoric monsters", and I also recall some crusty old bloke at a Yass petrol station warning me never to mess with a bungarra because "It'll run up ya."

These sinister words stuck in my mind for years. I could feel the steely sharp claws digging into my skull, my eyes popping like juicy, ripe grapes, the look of horror on bystanders' faces as they backed away from my pain-stricken cries for help. "Get it off me! Oh god its claws are penetrating my braaaaiiiiinnnnn!"

My mind whirling with these imagined horrors, I edged away from the bungarra on the washing machine - but - and I was almost disappointed - it didn't run up me, and instead made a stately departure through the front gate, strolling back to the bush with a dignified "Well I wasn't really interested in it anyway" air. I've put a dog dish and water tray out for it in the hope that this will encourage it to stay outside and we won't find it standing on Gary's chest in the middle of the night trying to suck the moisture out of his exposed eyeballs, or - because crazy stuff just seem to happen at our place - lying in the lounge pool watching TV with the dog, and the shark.

My favourite heat wave critter was the owl. It was the cutest thing you have ever seen. From my googling efforts I'm pretty sure it was a boobook - at any rate, it was small, and cross, because I disturbed it from its hideout behind the toilet cistern. It perched on my scooter and gave me a really dirty look, so I apologised and went inside, chastened, leaving the toilet and the laundry to the animal kingdom.

At least the animals have more common sense than some of the tourists who come into the roadhouse. "We are adventuring Mountain Augustus in tiny inadequate car! Is raining yes no?" I check out their car, which looks like a plastic Ken & Barbie accessory, and ask them if they have spare tyres, fuel and lots of water. "Yes we are of petrolising now and having shop of water!" they say as one of them fills up the weeny little 2.7

litre petrol tank and they each hold up the one small bottle of water that they've already started drinking before they've even left the store.

"You're all going to die," I explain. They smile and wave. "Ha ha! You are most humour, Ostrian lady!" They head out into the scorching sun, their flimsy fashion sandals melting on the bitumen, still waving and smiling, and I wave back. "We'll look for your desiccated corpses in a week or two! Have fun!"

Some days it seems that people just suddenly decide to leave home and drive into the outback without any planning, or thinking, or anything. "Which way is Newman?" "Is this Sandstone?" Can't people read? In the past eight hundred kilometres of driving, did it not occur to anyone to look at a map or - god forbid - look up from their phone facebook page long enough to read even one road sign? Then they scream because there's a single small frog in the public toilet. You have no idea, I think. Try using the bathroom at our place.

People wonder how we can stand it out here - the isolation and the heat, the flies, snakes and critters - but you soon discover that there's a stark beauty surrounding it all, secret places where you can swim and rest in the shade far from the city crowds, and instead of movie theatres, we have spectacular sheets of heat lightning revealing distant rainstorms and tree silhouettes on the far horizon. There's the relief of water on your thirsty skin in a mine pit pool as the sun goes down, the soft warm silence of the outback night, dragging your bed outside to watch tiny bats and shooting stars overhead, the almost-cool just before dawn. We spray-mist our trees to help the poor panting birds and put out water trays for the bungarras, putting up with all the frogs and snakes and creepy crawlies who, like us, just want some relief from the searing sun, and at the end of the day there's nothing like peeling your work shirt off under the struggling air con fan or sitting in the pool with the kids, the dogs, a cold beer and - look out! - a plastic shark.

when I'm ~~95~~ ~~70~~ ~~64~~ ?

This month I realised that I and my handsome personal donkey boiler constructor, Gary Hammer, are getting older at the terrifying rate of one year per annum, and - to our stunned disbelief - we will one day be Ancient, and possibly also Decrepit, although I think this may have already happened. Clearly it was time to check the piggy bank to make sure there are enough dollar coins, bottle tops and bits of fluff to cover the cost of our zimmer frames, plastic teeth and other lifestyle enhancements that we will need as various parts of our once-magnificent bodies continue to crumble away, so I tried one of those online calculators that works out how much money you need in order to retire. It said we needed at least 23.7 million dollars! Then we took the Learjet, private island, sultry Italian personal assistants and designer cocaine out of the budget, and it came up with just 5.3 million. Whew, what a relief!

We checked our bank account, and, to our astonishment, we don't have 5.3 million dollars. Do you? No. I didn't think so. Oh - hang on - Gaz says, if you do, could you spare us a quid? We can't pay it back, but you'll feel good about yourself, and if our legs are still working we can probably help take out the bin. I think we've earned something like 20 million over our lifetime so far, but we seem to have selfishly spent it on smokes, chocolate, books, motorcycles, getting drunk and having a good time. What idiots we were!

So, anyway, the online calculator was a bit of a disappointment, But we're still better off than my friend Jeremy, who was told by the calculator that "The amount you need to save exceeds your life expectancy." Jeremy said this was great because it meant there was no point in worrying about it any further and he could happily go back to fooling around with his guitar collection and living on lentils in between late night re-runs of Star Trek. You don't get that kind of financial advice from Mr. Boring Superannuation Planner at the bank, do you? I bet he doesn't even know who 7 of 9 is (episode 2008176).

Now, remember when superannuation first reared its beady, greedy, little eyes from the bubbling cesspit of governmental economic "planning" years and years ago? Remember how you kind of thought, in a glazed, oh-god-do-I-really-have-to-know-about-this kind of way, "Umm, this sounds too good to be true" and "Huh? Super an-yoo what? Get me a cold beer love will yer"?

I recall saying at the time, like many other Australians, "Ha ha, there's no way we'll ever see a cent of that money!" Even when it started, most of us could clearly see that it was just another scam dreamed up by the usual corporate sociopaths - if the government really wanted us to save for retirement, they would have set up a simple savings scheme, not gambling on the stock market (which is exactly what superannuation funds do, as many of us learned to our sorrow during the GFC). Remember how they told us that superannuation was being invented so that Australians would be covered in their old age as the pool of income-earning young people dwindles or wanders off to check their facebook page instead of going to work 23 hours a day the lazy b%@$#gers and the baby boomers began retiring in droves?

But - surprise! - now we're being told that we'll all probably have to work until we're 70 (or whatever they've put it up to this week), because there isn't enough money. That's right - even though the super funds have raked in absolutely squillions of dollars, there isn't enough to keep the oldies - us! - in tins of tuna and an occasional copy of the Tabform each week, let alone all the hip joints, teeth and colostomy bags we're going to need. Where did the money go? I'm with Pauline on that one: *Please Explain.*

Between the two of us, Gaz and I have something like 143 superannuation funds, each with about $1.65 in them (before fees). I think this is what they mean when they tell you to diversify your assets, although they are all diversified within the one stock market ("please explain"). You probably have the same financial situation. We're free to spend 97 hours a week "rolling over" our funds and filling out incomprehensible forms online - "simples!", as they say on the telly. We might have a little bit of trouble <u>finding</u> our super companies, though, because they keep changing their names every couple of weeks. Gary's original fund has been eaten by other super funds about 7 times in six years by my reckoning - they're hungry buggers, aren't they? We're building a totally separate shed for all the paperwork, and offering 13 tins of tuna a week to any retired person willing to keep it organised.

Now, for my entire working life I've paid heaps of tax, just like you, and every day I drive past the fruits of my labours - Centrelink, the Department of Housing, and all the other taxpayer-funded support services that look after the many people who need food, accommodation, child support and medical services just like the rest of us (even though some of us have to get drug-and-alcohol-tested in order to obtain our pay, while others appear to be given money in order to buy drugs and alcohol - but don't get me started on that one). In other words, we've worked our bums off and handed over a heap of dosh. A lot of us in Australia are unpaid volunteers and contribute priceless services every day.

So how come there's nothing left for you and me and Gaz when we need it? The super industry has collected literally BILLIONS and BILLIONS from us workers over the years, and I find it impossible to believe that there isn't enough to go around - Gaz and I are happy to not have annual "business trips" to China, glitzy conferences in exotic capital cities, new carpets and matching wallpaper in our office or private chauffeurs to our chartered helicopter, if that helps. We can just walk to the shop, and the dog can carry the Tabform and the cat food if we get a bit wobbly on the way back. We wouldn't mind the odd three-star motel holiday on the coast once in a while, but only if there's enough for old Mavis from round the corner to come too, she's been on her own for a while and it would do her a world of good.

Anyway, realising that we will probably be up the creek without the proverbial retirement-wise, and concerned about our state of future readiness, Gaz and I went and stared at our collection of baked beans and instant noodles, which we keep handy in case of an emergency. That's right - we're "preppers"! Except that unlike most preppers, the emergency we are prepared for is not nuclear war, ebola or an earthquake, but more along the lines of "Where's Matthew? Can't he go to the shop? My hips feel funny."

We counted up our stockpile, and worked out that we have enough food to last 9 hours if we feed the dog, 2.7 days if we don't feed the dog, and three weeks if we eat the dog (we're saving the cat for Christmas). It was immediately obvious that we don't have enough put away for next week, let alone retirement, and unless we could come up with a plan, desperate measures might be called for.

So here's the retirement plan that Gaz and I have worked out - anyone can do it, so why not share it with friends and family? It's cheap, simple, exciting, and - this is the best bit - the infrastructure, procedures and staff are already in place.

We're going to turn to a life of crime. Many have done so in the past, making a solid career out of it, even going on to become celebrities. The benefits are obvious. Why pay thousands of dollars a year at a retirement home when you can have fully supported accommodation, education, medical care, counselling and countless other opportunities in jail? You've already paid hundreds of thousands of dollars in tax, the jails are already built, and you don't have to go through a complicated and expensive application procedure. The only decisions you need to make are (a) what crimes you'd like to commit and (b) where you should commit them in order to maximise your chances of incarceration at the seaside minimum security prison of your preference. Or maximum security, if you prefer more privacy.

Our crime spree, when it comes, will be socially responsible - getting old is no excuse for not staying involved in the community and doing your bit. Our target: grey nomads. They've got insurance, and they could use the excitement. Imagine the blogging opportunities! Instead of comparing the toilet facilities at the 270 roadhouse stops they made across WA and how Fred tried to cut his hair with the nail clippers to save money until pension day, they can have blog entries such as, "Betty at site 12 was told to hand over the spare gas cylinder by an outlaw couple wearing home-made clown masks, one of them was on a zimmer frame with a sinister foreign accent. Fred saved us by hitting the tall, toothless one in the knees with the folding fishing seat, and then we all had a lovely hot cuppa while we waited for the police."

In contrast, in a nursing or retirement home, you have things like cheerful music therapists, who sit by your bed playing "Kumbayah" on the guitar, and your family are allowed to visit. In prison, there are no such abuses. There are the excellent deterrents of invasive personal searches, sniffer dogs and grim-faced guards wielding batons to keep annoying family members at bay, and dignified activities such as woodwork, TAFE courses, and fighting. As an elderly person in prison, you can easily defend yourself from any threatening cell mates.

"Now young feller, did I ever tell you about the time my old pop, back in '95 . . . or was it '96 . . . " *"It was 97, Bob"* "Stop interruptin a bloke Doris, anyway young feller it was back before the war . . . or just after the - - no it was during the sheep shortage . . . where was I?"

Anyhow, if you want to join our retirement gang, you're welcome. We'll be laying low somewhere with our getaway scooter, making papier-mâché handguns out of last week's Tabform and planning our next raid on the Leafy Haven Caravan Park. Synchronise your watches. Oh, and if you're coming through town, do you mind picking up a tin of tuna and something for the dog? We'll pay you back with food vouchers. We desktop-published them just this morning and the ink's nearly dry. Ta.

The following article made the regional ABC radio news, who rang to interview me about it one morning while I was collecting wood at our bush camp. I also provided the weather report for Meeka during the same interview; it made me feel well and truly like a "bushie".

I wrote this for The Meekatharra Dust in a sensationalist reporter style; here is a reformatted version, with some of the original photos and text that went with it. Big thanks and credit go to Matty, Splinter and Dave for the photos, and teamwork. Anal retentive bureaucratic types should note that the article & photos were put together here to be entertaining and is not a depiction of professional or volunteer emergency services protocols, so chill out and just enjoy the story.

INCHES FROM DEATH
LUCKY PUP SAVED BY PLUCKY CANUCK

> They say cats have nine lives, but Meeka dog Brayden must have had a couple of spares up his paw when he fell into Luke's Pit near the look-out on Sunday November 17.

By Over-The-Top Reporter Anna Johnson

Owner Matty Buist was taking Brayden down to the Luke's Pit swimming hole when the hapless hound decided to take a shortcut - right over the edge of the cliff.

Amazingly, Brayden survived the 25 metre fall but found himself trapped on a narrow ledge halfway down the pit wall. Matty swam the length of the pit and tried to climb up, without success. He enlisted the help of Dave Maly, who also attempted to scale the almost-sheer pit wall, but the deadly crumbling earth made it impossible - desperate, Matty rang 000.

A Sheila To The Rescue

Meekatharra S.E.S. Manager Splinter took the call, and rang Fire & Rescue Brigade Captain Gary Hammer to enlist the help of the brigade. As the team leaders debated which blokes with vertical rescue experience were available, it turned out to be wombat-shaped, middle-aged firefighter and reformed Canadian, Anna Johnson, who had the skills for the job.

"I'm fifty, fat, menopausal and terrified of heights," said Johnson. "But I'd done basic vertical rescue training and I'm also good with dogs - I was Brayden's best chance of making it out alive," said the modest matron.

Splinter put the SES winch truck in position as Gary and Dave strapped Anna into the rescue basket and secured the safety lines. Whimpering and afraid, Brayden watched from below as the team slowly winched Johnson down the rough cliff face. Displaced rubble rained down on the courageous Canadian as onlookers gathered at the lookout to watch the unfolding drama.

"Getting down was the easy part," said Johnson. "I just closed my eyes and tried to pretend I was on a nice sleigh ride back in the snowy lands of my childhood. It didn't work."

Up above, Splinter, Gary and Dave kept a close watch on the basket and lines, inching Anna down the perilous precipice.

Huddled against the cliff wall, Brayden watched anxiously as the basket finally reached the ledge.

"This was the most dangerous bit," said Johnson. "I could see Brayden was scared by me and the equipment. I was worried he would panic and back over the edge, so even though I just wanted to get the hell off that cliff, I had to take things real slow."

"Good Boy!"

With the frightened dog only two steps from a 25 metre fall to skull-shattering sharp rocks below, Johnson slowly coaxed Brayden forward and eased the safety strap around his chest.

"He was shaking and whimpering, but it was like he knew I was there to help him," said Johnson. "I used dog 'play' signals and kept telling him he was a good boy. Keeping him calm kept my mind off how scared I was myself."

With the petrified pooch securely strapped in, Anna gave the team up top the "all clear" signal, and they began the slow, gruelling ascent.

"It was much harder going up," reported Johnson. "The basket kept rocking and bumping on the rough cliff surfaces, and I only had one hand free to keep us steady - no way was I going to let go of that dog. There was a lot of debris tumbling down and I was hunched over to protect Brayden. He was so good - at one point he started to panic and wriggle, so I said 'Hey good boy, don't look mate', and he just stuck his head between my knees and closed his eyes!"

A Close Call

Johnson and Brayden were within inches of the cliff top when things suddenly seemed to go wrong: "I heard Gary and Dave yell out. The basket stopped, and then I heard someone call out for more rope," said Johnson. "Even though we had a safety line, I couldn't see what was happening, and I assumed the worst. Gary reassured me that everything was fine, but to me it sounded like in the movies where they use that fake cheerful 'we're going to be forced to helplessly watch you die and thank god you can't see how unbelievably bad it's going to be' voice, so I just kept talking to the dog and trying not to imagine the unravelling shreds of the safety lines slowly snapping one by one."

Heave Ho And Up She Rises

Up top, the blokes were securing the basket with an extra emergency line. As this is a family paper, we have substituted the blokes' colourful language with less graphic Aussie vernacular; your imagination can fill in the reality.

"As the basket came to the cliff edge, it got caught on a protruding section of rock, putting a strain on the basket and lines," explained handsome fire & rescue captain Gary Hammer. "Dave and I saw it at the same time and said "Oh, golly gosh!""

Deciding it would be safer to attach more safety lines to the basket and guide Johnson by hand around the obstruction, Dave called out to Splinter for "some more darn rope". With extra lines in place and cursing his lack of foresight in not shacking up with a stick-thin 40-kilogram supermodel, handsome harmonica player Hammer heroically hauled his hefty heartthrob from her precarious perch.

"Strewth crikey!" exclaimed the corpulent Canuck as she shakily emerged from the basket with the cowering canine. "Might want to put that dog on a diet."

Bermuda Triangle In Meeka ?

Safe at last in Matty's arms, Brayden offered generous slobbers of thanks to his rescuers, but there was more drama to come.

"Oh, sugar!" exclaimed Dave. "Me flippin' phone's fallen over the edge!" The team looked down in horror - was the mine pit some kind of outback Bermuda Triangle, sucking dogs and phones into its sinister depths?

"Dang it, now we won't be able to put it on You Tube," said Dave. There was only one solution - Captain Gary Hammer was winched down for an uneventful second recovery mission.

Disappointed by the lack of bone-crushing avalanches, blood or screaming, the look-out tourists headed off as the weary team packed up and made their way home for some well-earned cold beers and Schmackos.

Lessons Learned

Meekatharra is surrounded by open mine pits, and although they are protected by barriers and signs, Brayden's story shows just how easy it is for the unwary to get into trouble.

"We all learned something today," reflected handsome hero Gary Hammer. "Brayden's a lucky dog, and we hope that he's come away from this with a better understanding of mine pit safety."

SES Local Manager Splinter emphasised the vital role of Meekatharra's emergency services volunteers. "I'd like to thank everyone on the team. It's important that our townspeople can rely on us, whether it's a person or a dog. Calling 000 was the right thing to do in this situation, because we have the skills and resources to handle the risks. Our message is, 'Don't try this at home'".

Grateful owner Matty summed up the day's events with an emotional plea: "It's a lesson to all of us to educate our dogs about mine pit hazards. I can't thank the team enough for rescuing my best mate."

Asked for his comments, St. John Ambulance Volunteer Dave Maly replied with classic outback candour, which unfortunately is too graphic to print here.

And what about the daring diva of the day's drama? Asked if she'd do it again, the brave beaver-buster simply looked up from her foetal position curled around a cold beer and said, "Are you #@$%&*% kidding?"

Luke's Pit - Meekatharra's own Bermuda Triangle?

"I knew you'd save me, Dad!" Grateful Brayden slobbers thanks all over his rescuers. Despite his 25 metre fall, Brayden miraculously survived with just a few bruises - sadly, other dogs in the pit's past have not been so fortunate.
Photos by Matty, Splinter & Dave

home is where the toilet dump is

I know many people dream of hitting the road and seeing Australia, and as it's tourist season here in Meeka I thought I would pass on a few handy tips that you won't find on the grey nomad websites - I lived on the road in my old bus for a year or so and I learned a lot, so here are the bits I can still piece together after all the drinking and irresponsible behaviour (I was only 48 at the time).

First of all, don't dibble dabble around with some idea that you'll rent your place out while you "go travelling". Why add to your stress? Just sell everything you own and leave a note for the kids where they can find it when they come home from school to discover complete strangers renovating the kitchen, then hit the road. Forget about all the planning and anxiety that you encounter on the internet road-travel sites - they can be very useful, but trust me, you are not going to be attacked by sinister, drooling stalkers at isolated campsites or eaten alive by ravening snakes/dingos/bungarras in the ladies toilet. The only hazard I encountered was myself ("Let's get out those three whole bottles of tequila that I hid behind the Engel!") and some peculiar religious people at Hamelin Pool, but their god punished them by making their caravan break down and I was able to escape before I lost the thin veneer of polite behaviour I was struggling to maintain. Also there was the roo shooter, but that's a whole other story and horrifically unsuitable for a family newsletter.

Anyhow, you don't need the 7,358 items of Essential Equipment that some of the more zealous travelling websites like to recommend. The reason for this is that no matter where you go, there will be some retired bloke with way too much gear who will be ecstatically excited about the opportunity to use his trailer-load of equipment and, as a bonus, tell you off for Not Being Adequately Prepared as he sternly sets about fixing your vehicle while you relax and have a nice cuppa with the missus, who will be relieved to have a break from hearing about the fuel consumption charts and the most recent adjustments to the 12 volt wiring reverbolator thingamebob.

Despite all the tempting gadgets available at the satanically expensive caravan shops, the items I found most useful were books, a record player, a set of dog hair clippers, several buckets, a cat, a two-week supply of clean underwear, a couple of spare mugs, and not owning a house. The books and dog clipper were better than money for bartering in goods and services, Smokey kept the mice at bay on the rare occasions when he was fully awake (he's roughly 193 in cat years), and the spare mugs were handy for cups of tea for the curious passersby who wanted to visit my four-legged travel companions & check out my rig. "Is this your cubby house?" small children would ask, awestruck, before disappearing into the depths of the bus for hours, dressing Honey up in the snorkeling gear and completely reprogramming the portable TV. "You can get Foxtel in Chinese now. Can me and my brother live here with your dog?"

So, now that you're not prepared, where will you go? I strongly advise not having a plan - buy a cheap old bus that can be easily repaired with gaffer tape and bits of wood by any passing farmer, then wander off down secondary roads, dirt tracks & goat paths as they take your fancy - you'll be amazed at the rewarding adventures you'll have when your old rig breaks down in the middle of nowhere. Some of the best times I had on the road were when things went wrong. I was entirely at the mercy of whoever passed by, and it was great - I had to camp out in front of the mechanic's garage in Norseman for a week waiting for new tyres, and it was heaps more fun than staying in the caravan park at Esperance because I got to meet everyone in town as they came to see the bus, got offered native honey from the local beekeeper and helped catch the town's stray chihuahua in a scene reminiscent of something from The Benny Hill Show. This totally beat sitting around a jam-packed caravan park listening to my neighbours listing the pros and cons of every single shower block they used between Adelaide and Kalgoorlie and how Fred tried to save money by using nail clippers on his hair which is why they ended up at the nursing post in Emu Flat for a week.

Due to television, the biggest fear my friends and family had about my solo road life was serial killers - don't worry, they're not out there. They're at your house. Or next door. Statistics show you are more likely to be killed by someone who loves you, so obviously the best safety precaution is to leave your loved ones at home - after all, you can easily find new ones at most roadhouses, if you're not too fussy. But do take the dog - dogs don't argue about which turnoff to take, they're an excellent source of heat and, if you ocky-strap their front paws to the steering wheel, they can share the driving on the Nullarbor while you have a snooze and catch up with a few Star Trek episodes in the back.

On that note, keep in mind that driving across the Nullarbor is compulsory and heavy fines apply to any road travellers who fail to do so; make sure you take lots and lots of money and some spare internal organs or small orphaned child-workers that you can trade to pay the $23.75 per litre fuel prices and towing fee when your vehicle breaks down and you discover it will take 47 days for a new fuel pump to arrive. If you're quick you can usually snap up a tradable spare child or two from the back of the roadhouses where their stress-maddened parents have abandoned them at the 900 kilometre mark. An important safety precaution on the Nullarbor is not to travel with someone you know, because trust me, you will be ready to stab each other's eyes out with the plastic camping forks before you're even halfway across - remember, the word "Nullarbor" is Olde Latin for "Oh God Will This Never End Why Didn't You Buy More Cigarettes In Ceduna Like I Told You To".

What about the daily comforts - where will you shower, or blow dry your hair? Don't worry about it - as science tells us, you get used to your own body stench after three days and after that it's just a simple matter of standing downwind in close social situations. I know of one retired gentleman who solved the shower problem by simply using baby wipes. "Ain't had a shower in two years an I still smell clean and fresh! Yer might want to think about them disposable paper panties, yerself." (I'm not making this up). Personally, I opted to have a small shower, chemical toilet and proper underwear in my bus, which also features one-way tinted windows, making it possible to enjoy a leisurely shower in the Bunnings car park in Adelaide - one of the many handy highlights of mobile home living that is inexplicably never mentioned in tourism brochures, but is a unique and naughtily satisfying travel experience.

The escalating costs of caravan parks can easily be avoided by pulling up wherever you want to stay for the night, and rapidly consuming a lot of alcohol, so that if, for some bizarre reason, some official person ventures hundreds of kilometres into the outback to check on the thousands of informal overnight stops and attempts to "move you on", you can justifiably explain that you are too faarrghhn durrrgghh ha ha ha whoo! With the rates that caravan parks charge these days, it would take several bottles of spirits a night before the cost of drink-camping became a budget problem, so it's a good way of saving money while eradicating any annoying brain cells telling you it may not be such a good idea and why not get another bottle out from behind the Engel?

Another worry is security - how to protect your mobile dwelling when you're not in it? My own security system was rather lacking due to the age and condition of the bus, so I used to leave a hastily-scribbled note on the back of a used pie bag that read "SNAKE LOOSE IN BUS, HAVE GONE TO GET RANGER!!" I never had any problems, proving that this is an effective technique.

There are thousands of Australians living on the road either permanently or part-time; more and more people are escaping the mortgage trap and living the free-range life. I met nurses, teachers, carpenters, artists, retirees, terminally ill people, families, old ladies, young jack-of-all-trades blokes living in tents with their dogs, mad bikies with only a swag and one spare set of clothes to their name, Vietnam vets, psychologists, farmers, you name it - all living out of caravans, buses, tiny vans, utes and lord knows what else, working and travelling where and when they wanted. And whether they were in a fancy-pants million-dollar caravan or sleeping on a swag, everyone I met was *happy*.

Everyone helped each other out, and shared without thinking about it. If you looked like you needed a hand, you'd suddenly find a bunch of camping neighbours stepping in to help, everyone sharing a laugh and lending their gear, swapping each other for fresh fish and bush tomatoes. I gave a travelling farmer a haircut with the dog clippers in exchange for inflating my hilariously cheap rubber boat, then traded boat rides for fresh calamari with the elderly couple at the next camp. Honey and Smokey loved the road life, and we made friends at every stop, sometimes travelling in "tagalong" for a few days, then drifting apart to other adventures.

Living on the road rejuvenated me; all the madness that creep into us through the idiocy of television and city life slowly disappeared. By the time I rolled up in Meekatharra, my city demons had been replaced by a wonder at how many good people there are. The road and this crazy small outback town taught me how easy it is to just live, and be happy. Even if you have to share the spare teeth. Do you mind dropping them off next time you come into town? Gary promised Brian he could borrow them if Brian gives Steve that carton that Jason or Ben got from the party where the pig on a spit caught fire. I think. The one where Sarah backed into the beer esky with Shannon's ute. Or was it Shane? Was that the same night Greg had to take the kids home from the fire brigade social due to Tamika finding them barracking for Collingwood on the old telly we got from whatsisname's mate down at the railway dam camp in exchange for helping Sonja's friend set up the barbecue someone borrowed from Marcus and...where was I?

Anyhow, if you're ever in Meeka, why not say g'day? We're at the pub. Just keep going north past where the truck rolled over where the Bluebird mine used to be, next to where Uncle Colin nearly hit the cow, then keep going past the old iceworks and the spot where Narelle had the donut stand, where the powerhouse was and then just across from the pile of dirt.

Yer can't miss it.

Anna is currently working on her next collection of true stories entitled "Don't Squeeze The Cat".

No bungarras were harmed during the making of this book.

GLOSSARY

Translations of Australian words into English

mate	friend
arsehole	friend
bastard	friend
dickhead	friend
prick	friend
twat	friend
cunt	best friend
abos	derogatory abbreviation of 'aboriginal'
Aerogard	a type of tasty sauce that you spray on yourself to attract insects; tropical strength is good for attracting the larger insects
Akubra	the famous Aussie hat, but only to be worn once it has been trampled in a stampede, washed down the creek, mauled by a dingo and left in the sun for five years or so
arse	a person's bottom, 'ass', also used as an insult, as in 'arsehole'
barbie	barbecue; a food preparation technique involving beer, men, and fire
beanie	knitted cap worn in cold weather, i.e. below 35°C
betadine	like iodine - a stinging antiseptic liquid men won't let women put on their roo-gutting knife injuries, minor scrapes etc because it is, apparently, more painful than childbirth
Bindie	the famous Meekatharra post office dog & sandwich stealer
bindies	spiny seed balls that stick to skin, clothes, dogs, bloody everything, especially Gary's socks and if he puts them in the wash like that again he'll jolly well hear about it you mark my words
bloke	male human, usually found in pubs or around the backs of utes; when sober can be generally useful around the house, shed etc
blue	calm, rational discussion between articulate, sensitive adults
blunnies	'Blundstone' ankle-high work boots, or boots that resemble them, worn by men, women, children, with work clothes, dresses, pyjamas, bathers, or nothing at all
bungarra	monitor lizard or goanna, usually quite large, often found in our bathroom, very tasty & popular menu item in W.A. If you find one dead at the side of the road, why not take it home for a tasty dinner treat? It tastes like chicken. Sort of.

Bunnings	horribly addictive hardware store chain from which there is no escape; Australians are not allowed to leave the store unless they have purchased more items than will actually fit in their car
bush bike	bicycle or motorcycle that can handle being ridden in 'the bush', usually something unlicenced and too bashed up for road use, or one that was perfectly all right until you took it bush like Mum said not to
bush tucker	food obtained from 'the bush', i.e. natural indigenous food, including animals such as kangaroo, bungarra, snakes, witchetty grubs etc
bustard	tall, stern-looking native bird with long legs and creepy eyes
carton	24 cans of beer (compulsory daily per head consumption in W.A.)
cattle dog	blue or red heeler, the classic Aussie work dog, very intelligent and keen, can drive a ute, radio for help, fly the station helicopter -- oh, no, that's Skippy the bush kangaroo, anyway real good dogs mate, ask Roy if he's got any from that last litter and give him a carton for it
chook	chicken; also a term of endearment or insult, depending on mood
clobber	clothing, or whatever is lying handy on the dirt floor of your camp
cogla	bush banana, bush pear - an indigenous wild fruit that grows on vines
Commie	Commercial Hotel, open most days, come on in, say hi to Meacho
Coolgardie safe	brilliant Australian evaporative cooling system - box with wet burlap, keeps food cool for up to 5 minutes
copper (1)	olden times - large copper vessel for boiling clothes, horse parts etc
copper (2)	police officer, not fooled by your poorly-thought-out excuses
crikey	cockney/Australian slang that no one knows the meaning of, used to express surprise or when confronted by member of Irwin family
cuppa	cup of tea or coffee, if beer not available
divvy van	police van, many locals' home away from home
dog box	small, hot room in a donger that you wouldn't keep a dog in but may be appealing to women if you stand in the doorway in a pair of filthy underpants and offer them enough beer, apparently
donger	transportable shipping container-like building at the back of remote roadhouses, camps etc. in which outback men are stored overnight until needed for work
donkey boiler	outdoor water container over a fire, for hot water, come back in a few hours to find out it's gone out or ruptured and wash yourself with a rag and stick instead or just not bother until next Sunday
double-gees	incredibly tough, sharp spiny seed, can go through tyres, the main reason you'll see kids riding bikes with no tyres on them; can also be sold to tourists as 'thorny devil lizard eggs' - yes the genuine article

	mate, they charge an arm and a leg for em in the city but I'll let yer have em for just a tenner mate orright no worries righto Nige let's go to the pub
dugite	extremely poisonous snake which enjoys sleeping in our bathroom
elders	older indigenous people, community leaders, able to talk with you without checking Facebook every minute
Engel	brand of portable electric fridge which Australian men fill with beer, kangaroo meat and fish, putting the milk and the rest of the food on the fold-out bed to go off then complaining about the smell
esky	insulated plastic box for carrying beer and ice; it is compulsory for all Western Australians to carry at least one full esky at all times
FIFO	fly-in, fly-out; also called 'fly in, fuck off' - a term that describes visiting mine workers who are flown in and out of mine camps, losing touch with their families and neighbourhoods back home, and generally not able to take part or spend money in the mining town community, hence the derogatory perception by townspeople
flats	a randomly-nominated flat area of land that everyone agrees to call 'the flats' or 'the flat' in order to distinguish it from the other flat areas surrounding it in every direction
footy	Australia's official religion - Australian rules football; it is a federal offence not to join in a discussion of footy at all times in season
genny	generator; used everywhere in the outback as power source and coveted by all outback blokes; excellent conversation topic at parties; must never be called by its full name, more interesting when broken
Gero	Geraldton, a town south of Meekatharra where there are shops, traffic lights, people who wear shoes etc.
gidgie, gidgee	type of hardwood tree commonly found throughout the outback, old and twisty-looking, ash is burned to mix with chewing tobacco
ging	slingshot weapon popular with outback kids, responsible for untold damage to windows, native animals, illegal in most areas
grey nomads	retired people travelling in caravans or motorhomes, generally carrying more equipment than an Antarctic expedition
grog	alcohol
gwarda	poisonous snake that no one can agree on what it looks like
Hills Hoist	a spinning stand-alone laundry line; Australian invention created so that children can hang off it and go round and round and round until your sister throws up and it breaks and jeez Mum's gunna go off at ya
icy pole	popular frozen ice confection which lasts about 3.1 seconds in average outback summer conditions

jumper	sweater; worn when freezing conditions below 40°C occur
lamingtons	deceptively light sponge cake that doesn't taste good with beer
Landor	remote outback station where annual horse races are held and your mates drink way too much, throw up and fall into the creek
lolly	candy
loo	toilet, bathroom, popular with snakes, mice, spiders etc
mermaids	truck inspectors, or something, who knows
metho	methylated spirits, emergency alternative to beer
midgie	small biting insect like a mosquito
missus	woman you are in trouble with, i.e. wife, partner, usually angry
Mortein	chemical spray that causes Meeka insects to mutate into monsters
musos	people who convince others that they are musicians in order to get free beer; also, your mates after drinking lots of beer and deciding to sing "Smoky Train" over and over and over and...
musterin	mustering - rounding up livestock so you can have your steak; a filthy, exhausting season of work unless you are Lauren and wearing pearl earrings and able to look fresh & fabulous even after wrestling entire cows to the ground with your bare hands
nappies	diapers, second most common source of littering after red cans
nah	Australian noise meaning 'no', but usually used in conjunction with the word 'yeah', as in "Yeah, nah, mate, yer want the 2.5 mill not that piece of shit tell Davo to give yer the one off his Landy"
ocky-strap	elastic straps used for tying down gear on cars and taking your eye out when it disintegrates and snaps in the outback sun
paddock basher	old vehicle used off-road or around the station, usually for fun by people drinking beer
Panadol	popular headache tablet taken after drinking beer
patch	your personal prospecting spot, unless Grunter spots it first
pavlova	very sweet meringue dessert with fruit and cream, never turns out looking like the photo in the cookbook unless you are 76 years old and called Mavis
piss	alcohol, consumed in such vast personal quantities in WA that you "piss it out", hence the charming nickname
pub	a hotel bar that provides alcohol and food, where you go to "hang shit" on your mates or fight with them over a sheila
RACV	roadside assistance service for car owners in state of Victoria, where, unlike W.A., you can break down in your car and not die

red cans	Emu beer cans, which cover about 99% of W.A.
rego	registration (Australians are incapable of using full words)
resto	restoration, usually in relation to a car that you will never actually get round to restoring but you like talking about it
road train	truck pulling one or more freight trailers, which locals hope will roll over so they can scavenge its frozen sirloin strips in the dead of night
roadhouse	garage with food, supplies, mechanical assistance, annoyed women
root	sexual intercourse, if you can call it that
shagging	sexual intercourse (see above)
skink	small friendly lizard, likes living rooms, dog food, sleeping on sofa etc
slab	24-pack of beer cans
smoko	smoke break, morning or afternoon tea break, snack
soak	a place where water accumulates to form soggy ground or perhaps some standing water
station	Australian equivalent of a ranch, also called homestead
stockman	similar to cowboy, someone who works with cattle and horses; in Australia there is a strong tradition of aboriginal stockmen, and the word unfortunately leaves out the many women who also do this job
strewth	cockney/Australian slang, "God's truth", now considered old & corny
stubbies (1)	Australian shorts worn by men, usually without underpants, awful
stubby(2)	bottle of beer (if you are ever mystified by an Australian word or saying, you can safely assume it has something to do with beer)
swag	rolled-up camping mattress with a tough canvas cover and snakes in it
ta-ta lizard	small, quick lizard that raises one front leg as if saying goodbye
texta	ink felt pen
the bush	nature - anywhere outside town
Tim Tams	addictive Australian chocolate-covered biscuit (cookie) that people fight over and try to hide from each other
tin opener	can opener, when a rock and a knife aren't handy
tip	dump - where people take their garbage, and you go and take it home
track	any unpaved road or barely-visible tyre tracks that may lead to a main road, water or certain death when you realise you're lost
tradie	tradesperson, can be found at the pub on Friday, otherwise forget it
truckies	truck drivers, famous for eating meals stacked high with 7 different types of animal, plus eggs and chips

tucker	food, consumed in order to maintain beer-drinking energy levels
uni	university; a place where 'gay wankers' go to learn 'fuckin bullshit'
ute	utility vehicle, single or twin cab, with a tray on the back, around which it is a legal requirement for men to gather when stopped
vegies	vegetables; dangerous, nasty-tasting things that should be fed to the dog when the missus isn't looking
woman	adult person doing 27 things at the same time while annoyed/hot, usually found surrounded by people not thinking
willy-willy	small, sudden outback tornado
Wiluna	small desert town whose entire population makes a regular exodus to Meekatharra for court day, drinking and fighting
wombat	slow, hairy, barrel-shaped marsupial and pretty much how you feel at the age of fifty when it's hot and you reach Peak Menopause
yakka	work

If any glossary terms are missing, you can safely assume that they are probably a term related to beer, amusing bodily functions, or generators.

For further explanations of the Australian language, just drop in to Meekatharra sometime for a yarn at the pub - visitors are always welcome, and we're a friendly mob. I'll have a Crownie, and Nige here will have a Fosters. Ya got any smokes?

Thinking Of Visiting Meekatharra?

Recommended Reading

Feel The Fear And Do It Anyway	Susan Jeffers
Escape To Nowhere	Amar Bhushan
Heart of Darkness	Joseph Conrad
S.A.S. Survival Handbook	John Wiseman
Championship Street Fighting	Ned Beaumont
Why Isn't My Brain Working?	Datis Kharrazian
The Call of the Wild	Jack London
Australia's Most Deadly and Dangerous Beasts	Bruce Thomson
Hunting, Butchering and Cooking Wild Game	Steven Rinella
Eat Meat and Stop Jogging	Mike Sheridan
Should I Stay Or Should I Go?	Lundy Bancroft
Women Who Think Too Much	Susan Nolen-Hoeksema
Why Men Don't Listen	Edward Ryan
How To Set His Thighs On Fire	Kate White
Mating In Captivity	Esther Perel
Politically Incorrect Parenting	Nigel Latta
Angry All The Time	Ronald T Potter
Sentenced To Hell	Natalie Welsh

www.ingramcontent.com/pod-product-compliance
Lightning Source LLC
Chambersburg PA
CBHW030936090426
42737CB00007B/446